Designing

A

HOME

INTERIOR DESIGN FOR
YOUR MODERN HOME

A ROOM-BY-ROOM GUIDE

Amy Landry

Contents

INTRODUCTION

How many times have you played with your imagination dreaming of designing a new home? If now the time has come to make this dream come true, you will be realizing how many things there are to consider.

Y ou will have to evaluate every single aspect of the spaces available, and in many cases, you will have to enlist the help of a designer or an interior designer. This short guide was created to enlighten you along the way of interior design and beyond. Let's find out together how to design a house, even on your own!

THE IMPORTANCE OF A DEFINED PROJECT

When you start thinking about how to renovate your home, it is essential to have a clear idea. When creating a new project, you will have to carefully evaluate every detail without leaving anything to chance.

Where to start? Obviously from your needs. Before you get down to business, ask yourself a few questions:

HOW MANY ROOMS WILL YOU NEED?

Is it finally time to build a second bathroom to transform into your personal oasis of relaxation?

Is the family about to expand and would you like a room for the future baby?

It will be your job to identify priorities, transfer them to paper and finally make them take shape in reality. Designing a house is not an activity that takes place every week. So don't forget anything, because once the work has started it will be almost impossible to apply changes to the project, unless you want to continue to lighten your wallet.

After personal needs, the second element that must be taken into consideration will undoubtedly be the budget. Anyone would like to be able to insert any option within their own home to obtain unparalleled living comfort, but unfortunately each of us has limited resources. Therefore, identify your fundamental objectives in which to invest: there will be time for everything else in the future!

Home design: where to start?

As we have seen above, designing a house originates from one's own needs and the available budget. Starting from these two pillars, the next step will be "saving what can be saved".

Each house has its own peculiarities and strengths. Why not make them functional also for the new look of your home? Let's say that in your home there is an old brick fireplace, or a mosaic that has remained intact over time. It will be time to give all these components a new life by harmonizing them with the future style of your design.

Before starting with the design of the new interiors it will be essential to take into consideration everything that is not visible, that is the state of the systems (plumbing, heating, electrics). You absolutely must not neglect this aspect. Designing a house without carefully evaluating the systems means meeting new renovations in the not-too-distant future that will nullify the work done up to that point.

Once the "systems" practice has been completed, you will need to choose the new design to give to your home. The style choices can be varied: classic furniture, Nordic style, country chic look ... decide which of these you like best and keep it as the leitmotif of the whole house. The guideline to follow in the choice of furnishings is that of harmony between all the accessories present. Imagine your home as a large orchestra in which each room will play its own instrument in unison with the other spaces.

The first accessories to choose will be the so-called fixed furnishings. With these we refer to the kitchen, the walk-in closet and all those furnishings that, once positioned, you will never move. Precisely because of their immobility, the evaluation and choice of the points in which to place them must be carried out with particular attention. The arrangement of the furniture will revolve around these.

In the creation of new home spaces, another imperative will be that of optimization. You must not create unnecessary clutter, and rather than parcel out the environment with corridors and small rooms it will be better to focus on open spaces. Optimizing space means above all maximizing living comfort.

So far, we have seen how designing a house is by no means an operation to be taken lightly. Often all you can do is seek advice from a professional, such as an architect or an interior designer.

However, even these consulting experts will appreciate a graphical representation of your ideas. How to recreate them? Fortunately, technology comes to our aid. On the web there are many free applications that will allow you to design a house with a few simple clicks. Design software will shape your interior ideas. These programs will surely be useful to remove any doubts about the furniture to use: seeing your fantasies projected on the screen you will visually understand if they are actually for you or not.

Do you prefer pen and paper? Create a floor plan of the house to scale and try to figure out how to arrange the furnishings. You can also design

a single plant for each room, creating a mood board to inspire you: clippings from furniture magazines, photographs, color palettes ... insert what you like, evaluate which combinations are the best, reflect on the style that would best reflect your personality and start the work!

The house is usually a place of relaxation and tranquility, where we spend a good part of our life, with our family or even alone and therefore it is a good idea, obviously if you have the possibility, to create your own spaces and environments in detail and with precision, every little detail that can be expressed.

Designing a house is a requirement that you may have when you are dealing with a new construction or with a renovation.

There are many points to face and decisions to make starting with the perimeter of the house, passing through the assignment of the rooms up to the choice of furniture.

What kind of perimeter do you want your home to have?

Before choosing the perimeter and the shape that your house will be, it is important to understand how many rooms and square meters we will need and if we want it on one floor or on several floors.

Let's take as an example the house that has a rectangular perimeter; our tastes may be different, however, and maybe we might want an L-shaped house, or a long and narrow house or a short and wide one; in short, the variables are really many. Here are a couple of them, to give you some ideas:

Rectangular perimeter

If we have chosen a rectangular perimeter, a possible variant is to have an entrance that leads us directly to the living room through a small hallway.

The house offers a lot of available space, for example, the room used as a living room adjoins the kitchen and a terrace; it has two entrances, one from the living room and one from the kitchen.

Behind the kitchen lies the sleeping area and the two bathrooms, thus giving a greater feeling of privacy, intimacy and confidentiality.

A rectangular house allows us to play better with spaces, providing us with many more variables of arrangement, this factor can satisfy more tastes and offer greater customization. Summarizing the house, we see present: a kitchen, a very large living room, a private room that can become a study or another bedroom, two bathrooms, two bedrooms and two terraces.

L-shaped perimeter

A house with an L-shaped floor plan leaves least room for customization.

The idea shown in the plan here is to arrange a part of the sleeping area on the right side of the house, positioning the entrance in the corner in order to gain space and already have a view of the whole house.

In front of the entrance there is the large living room, which has a kitchenette on the left, while on the right two small terraces.

Behind the living room there are two bedrooms, divided by a bathroom, which in turn have two terraces.

While the left side of the house boasts more rooms but much less large, in fact it consists of a closet used as a laundry room, a bedroom, a bathroom and a large veranda and a small terrace.

This house has: three bedrooms, a kitchenette, a living room, five balconies, a veranda, two bathrooms and a laundry room.

Questions to ask yourself before carrying out the interior design in your home

Having clear ideas about the renovation of the interior project is basic. Therefore, it is really important to know how to ask certain questions, in order to be of help to the interior designer. Usually, the issues to consider are the following:

Knowing your own needs or requirements that led you to want a new interior project;

Knowing the dimensions of the rooms, in the case of a simple renovation. Therefore, possess the floor plan of the house;

Your favorite style of furniture and that of all the members of the family that lives there;

Desired interior design for the whole house or for a single room, for example: bathroom, bedroom, study, living room, kitchen, etc.

Know the presence of particular elements or particular structures that could affect the work, for example: fixed furniture already present, pillars in awkward positions, stairs etc.

Know the colors you like and the ones you would like to avoid for walls and furniture;

Have the budget to be able to pay for the services performed by the interior designer or the architect.

Know how much budget you have available for the purchase of various furnishing and renovation materials.

Be sure that a 2D project is enough, or choose a 3D project, as the latter has the ability to demonstrate the rendering of the projects in a realistic version even before they are actually realized.

How to contact and whom, for the realization of the projects

If you are not an expert in the sector and do not know how to design a house, it is inevitable that you have to rely on an interior design professional, be it an architect or interior designer. Even the online architect is in fact the same professional that we will find in a classic technical studio and that designing a house online or even the interior of the house is an operation that can be easily performed remotely. Today, with a little imagination, but above all with a lot of time to spend, patience and a certain financial availability, you can design the type of house you most want, using 2D or 3D design programs or otherwise made with the help from these professionals.

To obtain an interior project with online design, relying on a real professional, it will be necessary to contact an interior design portal, making sure that it is authoritative, secure and has been online for several years, demonstrating its reliability.

If, on the other hand, we wanted to opt for a professional from a classic technical office but don't know anyone, just perform a search on Google.

Attention and beware of free interior design:

This advice is to be considered valuable: free interior design does not exist just as there is no free online interior design. When you search the web about online interior design you might run into fake websites or professionals offering free 3D interior design and free online interior design services.

No registered professional, after many years of studies or sacrifices, with a technical office, daily expenses, taxes to be paid, would carry out projects for the home for free, without any financial compensation.

Advice on how to make your home unique and dreamy

Play with the light: it is wonderful to admire the effect of the light passing through the windows of the house; in fact, the right lighting of each environment and the correct temperature in the rooms are really essential to make it as comfortable as possible. Focus on large windows that give the desired view that you have around the house. Here the luck of where you have chosen to live plays a large part; sea, mountain, plain, countryside, hill, city etc.

Good taste, first of all: it is not absolutely necessary to have works of art to decorate and furnish your home, but objects of a certain delicacy are enough, such as books, photos and various family memories and some design objects, alternating between them, to bring a carefully balanced whole.

Combinations: whether it is used to create inserts capable of highlighting a specific piece of furniture, or to recreate new color combinations, when designing a room, never be afraid to dare. Have fun combining the various materials through various insights that inspire you. For example, by associating the warmth of wood with the cold beauty of marble or materials such as iron, plastic and resins, you will obtain a balanced combination capable of spreading decorative potential.

Play with colors: the choice of colors can often appear to be a difficult moment, which ones can fit well on a single facade or in an entire room; but it is very important, as the color we choose particularly highlights all the details of the same room, highlighting the spaces and light points present. One piece of advice is to think carefully about the function you want to give to the room and its purpose, also based on your preferences of course. By means of this, you decide whether you prefer it to suggest warmth, have a relaxing atmosphere or be the most eye-catching room in the house.

Caution on cladding: the very first important notions to keep in mind so that the external cladding of your home is excellent are; functionality, aesthetics and protection. To realize these three objectives, the materials that are used for a facade must have certain properties, that is; durability, creative flexibility, resistance to UV rays, rain, adverse weather conditions, certified fire resistance, easy maintenance and repairability, and reliable structural performance.

Focus on the stairs: whether they are natural, in wood, steel, light or heavy, in masonry, glass, cantilevered or not, the stairs circumscribe the character of the house itself. This architectural constituent plays an indispensable function in the preparation of rooms on several levels, not only as an essential condition of vertical connection between the various floors, but also for the ability it has to enrich, refine or upset the appearance of the rooms. For example, if the interior architecture is the body of a building, the internal staircase is its heart.

Use various plants and flowers also: you absolutely must not forget them when you decorate the spaces, whether they are outside or inside, as they can give us an extra touch of life as well as having a real purification function for the air that circulates inside every room, continuously offering oxygenated and purified air.

Renew before changing: if you are already tired of an environment that is always the same and you believe it is absolutely necessary to make changes to diversify it, before investing time and money perhaps unnecessarily in new expenses or purchases, instead try to alter the

arrangement of what is already present inside a room. The advice therefore is to move the objects from their usual position, change the combination of the paintings on the walls. It only takes a little inspiration to give a new meaning and fresh air to a room.

Managing outdoor spaces: space is never actually enough whether one lives in a villa or an apartment; however, there are several tricks to create elegance and functionality even in the most confined spaces. For example, they sometimes believe that to be able to afford a swimming pool outside your home, or in a hypothetical garden, it is essential to boast of a lot of available space; in reality, this is not the case, since even smaller pools can be perfectly supported by smaller patios, terraces, gardens or courtyards. When it comes to swimming pool design, nowadays, there are a varied number of shapes, types, materials, coatings and sizes. Furthermore, they are perfect all year round, as, for example, an outdoor swimming pool can be used and heated even in winter; alternatively, it can be designed with the dual function of serving as a spa. They are, moreover, convenient, since the size of small and compact pools counts, as they allow for rapid and effective heating and the management costs to be faced are lower than those of a larger pool. They also add a defining point to the garden, making it aesthetically interesting; as they can have water features integrated into the design: for example, waterfalls or walls on which water flows. They are worth a lot, economically speaking, considering that if well done, an outdoor pool increases the house's value. Moreover, they are suitable for the whole family, to spend precious time there and enjoy it. They keep you fit and have healing powers; you don't need an Olympic-size swimming pool to keep fit and do some healthy exercise, but you can do both aerobic and resistance exercises even in a simple and small outdoor pool.

Here's how to design your home in 7 steps

1. STUDY THE STARTING SITUATION

"I want to design my house". It happens to everyone to think so. After all, our home is the place of affection, pleasure, rest: it has a huge impact on the quality of our lives. If you have also expressed this desire, here you will find the essential information on how to design a house, for free, on your own.

First of all, start by analyzing the starting situation: this will have an inevitable impact on the project. In short, to reach the finish line, you must first prepare yourself. So, answer these questions.

Do you want to build a house from scratch or renovate an existing house?

Do you want to design interiors or exteriors?

Is it a single house, an apartment, a semi-detached house or something else?

Where is the house? In the countryside or in the city? What are the characteristics of the place?

What are the bureaucratic requirements to be fulfilled?

Does your project comply with the regulations (PRG, municipal urban plan, landscape restrictions...)?

Is the project feasible? Is it economically sustainable?

If you want to design your home completely independently, you need to be aware of all the factors that will affect your desires, your programs, your needs. Even if you need to hire a professional to help you.

2. FIND IDEAS AND INSPIRATION

To create your home, you need to be a good observer. Look around you: what do you like about other people's homes and what do you dislike? You can look for ideas for home design in many ways: doing research on the internet, reading books and trade magazines, looking at the work of architects and interior designers.

3. DESIGNING A HOUSE FROM SCRATCH: THE STRUCTURE

Let's say you own a building plot and want to know how to design a house from scratch. What you need to do is to carefully follow these 4 essential steps.

Define the structure of the house: decide the shape and size; choose how many levels it must have (1, 2 or more), if there is to be a basement; think about the style you want to adopt, for example modern or rustic.

Define the internal subdivision: identify how to arrange the rooms, the dimensions and what functionality you want for each environment.

Prepare a rough project: draw the exterior of the house on paper or in 3D, decide the plans it must have, the appearance of the facades and outdoor spaces.

Switch from the sketch to the technical drawings: prepare the official documents of the house project, those that will have to be delivered to the competent offices to start the work.

To prepare the technical drawings (orthogonal projections with plan, elevation and section) it is necessary to make technical calculations relating to the safety and functionality of the structure (foundations,

floors, walls ...), but not only that. Imagine that you represent the building on a scale of 1: 100 exactly.

4. CHOOSE THE MOST SUITABLE CONSTRUCTION MATERIALS

When planning a home, decisions must be made that will affect the family's lifestyle, the performance of the building, and will also determine future expenses. So it is extremely important to choose wisely how to build or renovate the house: with which technique and with which materials?

You can rely on the usual method of brick houses. The building materials are the classics: reinforced concrete, bricks or stones, steel. Or you can build a prefabricated house out of wood, concrete, steel and glass.

Designing a house today means above all thinking about the safety of those who live there and the surrounding environment. Here, for example, is what you shouldn't give up:

- anti-seismic construction;

- high energy efficiency or self-sufficiency;

- durability and adaptability;

- space optimization;

- respect for the environment, soil and resources.

If you like to keep up with the times, you could consider green architecture and ecological houses: it would be a gain for the wallet and other things.

5. EVALUATE FACILITIES AND TECHNOLOGIES

This stitch is double-tied to the previous stitch. When designing the safety and functionality of the accommodation, make sure that the choice of facilities is consistent with your goals. In summary: choose between a traditional home or a smart home.

Do you prefer underfloor heating or radiators? Are you planning to install solar panels or photovoltaics? Do you want home automation, control systems from your smartphone or with automatic programming? Are you looking for traditional wooden window frames or do you want something ultra-modern?

The questions are endless, but only you can pinpoint them and find an answer.

6. DESIGNING THE INTERIOR OF A HOUSE

Deciding on your own how to design the interior of the house is perhaps a simpler task. There are many digital systems that can come to your aid. You can design the house in 3D with free or paid simulators. You can find them in the form of online sites, computer programs or apps for smartphones and tablets.

For DIY interior design the most used tool is the Ikea planner. If you are looking for valid alternatives, you could try Sketchup and SweetHome 3D (software), Homestyler Interior Design (app) and the program par excellence Autocad, available for PC and mobile devices.

The programs to design the house, the interiors and the furnishings give a realistic vision of the environments, and this allows you to make a conscious configuration of the spaces.

With the floor plan of the house in hand, do the interior design of the house following this list.

Number of interior spaces, type and size: living room, lounge, kitchen, bathrooms, bedrooms, basement, study, hobby room and so on.

House style: classic, modern, rustic, industrial, shabby chic, country, minimal, etc.

Room colors and themes: choose the color palette for each room, the materials such as tiles or wallpaper, the themes and shades of the furniture.

Type of furniture: fitted walls, bookcases, lounge furniture, kitchen furniture, bathroom fixtures, beds, bedroom furniture, various furnishing accessories and decorations.

Systems: for example, lighting, heating and air conditioning, video surveillance systems, alarms, home automation devices ...

7. DESIGNING THE EXTERIOR OF A HOUSE

How do you design a garden? To do exterior design, imagine the services you would like.

You may need a parking space, or an external garage. Maybe you have space to build a swimming pool. You may want a vegetable garden and an equipment shed. Perhaps you would like a well-kept lawn and garden to grow plants and flowers. You might like the idea of a gazebo, pergola, porch or terrace. Decide what you want to achieve and identify the ideal outdoor spaces for each service.

THE ENTRANCE

How to design the entrance by optimizing the spaces

The entrance to a house is its business card. For this reason, it must be designed with the same attention dedicated to the other rooms of the house.

Oscar Wilde said: There is no second chance to make a good first impression.

Starting from this quote we can understand how important it is in everything to carefully organize what reaches our guest in the first instance.

A well-designed entrance is a great business card.

In colder countries, the entrance is anticipated by a filter space.

The genkan is the entrance area of a Japanese house where you can leave your shoes.

The entrance is often used as a pocket emptier.

The entrance must be well lit even with artificial lighting systems.

So, let's try to see together how we can give importance to this space of the house.

House entrance project according to Feng Shui

Feng Shui also agrees that the design of the entrance to the house is fundamental. In fact, according to this art, it is one of the most delicate areas of the house, which, if well thought out, promotes the well-being and health of the inhabitants.

According to Feng Shui it is advisable that the entrance door opens towards the inside of the house, to give a sense of greater welcome. Also, the best orientation for the entrance door is the Southeast, as it is influenced by good energy.

Furthermore, it is good to have a wide entrance, in order to guarantee a sense of protection and comfort to those who enter. If there are more than one door, it is better that they all open in the same direction, to avoid creating disorientation.

If the door opens onto a blind wall, in order not to give a sense of claustrophobia, it is preferable to lighten this with a mirror or wall decoration.

The entrance of the house in other cultures

There are some cultures that have a special focus on the entrance space.

For example, in Scandinavian architecture, or in any case in colder countries, before the entrance there is a filter space, like a porch, in which overcoats and shoes are stored.

The same trick, but for mainly hygienic reasons, is also used in Japanese houses, where at the beginning of the house there is the genkan, a space where you can leave your shoes to put on the slippers provided by the owners of the house.

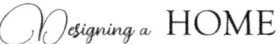

Home entrance projects: things to do and what to avoid

We now come to some tips on how to design an entrance.

There are, first of all, the things to avoid:

Storage mirrors

Make sure that there are not many doors opening off the entrance, because such a condition could generate disorientation, giving the idea of a real labyrinth.

Overfilling the space with furniture or using too dark colors, creating a stuffy and impractical environment.

The entrance opening onto a blind wall; if it cannot be avoided then, as we have seen, a mirror or a picture on that wall can correct this problem.

Make sure that the entrance doesn't open onto a long corridor; if this is unavoidable, we must try to break the rhythm, with decorations, niches and curtains for example.

Instead, what you need to do is:

As far as possible, favor the eastern position of the entrance, as it is the one in which the sun rises in the morning and therefore from which the best energy enters.

Filter the cold coming from the outside if you live in cold areas or the excessive heat if you live in too hot areas, by creating porches and verandas.

Illuminate the environment well, making extensive use of natural light, but integrating it with artificial lighting.

Having said that, we can find ourselves faced with various types of entrances; among these we propose some case studies in the following projects.

CLOSED ENTRANCE

In this renovation project, the original corridor was very long and the rooms were all placed in a row. Given the need to have a first room separate from the rest of the house, the corridor was reduced, so that it constituted only a sort of hallway between the area of the house intended for the study.

SEMI-OPEN ENTRANCE

This second solution has a semi-open entrance, with one side closed by a door leading to the sleeping area and one side open to the living area.

In this case, moreover, one side of the entrance was used to create a built-in wardrobe to be used as a wardrobe for the inhabitants and guests.

ENTRANCE TO THE ENVIRONMENT

In contemporary homes it is very easy to find entrances that give directly onto an environment with a different function, such as the living room or the kitchen.

This is the case, for example, in this project, where an attempt was made to give the entrance a definition, by inserting a transparent dividing element and a console with mirror and coat hanger on one wall.

ENTRANCE WITH STAIRCASE

Finally, we want to offer you an entrance with a staircase, in which the space under the stairs can be fully exploited by closing it with flush doors.

Alternatively, you can keep this space open, especially if the entrance is already quite narrow, furnishing it for example with a console and mirrors chosen ad hoc, in steel and ash.

Or you can opt for the more minimal one, which with its integrated LEDs can illuminate dark areas such as an area under the stairs.

HOW TO MAKE THE MOST OF THE ENTRANCE TO THE HOUSE

The examples proposed have already indicated the possible uses that an entrance can have, to avoid it being only an anonymous and neglected passage area.

Certainly, the most associated use of this space in the house is that of a wardrobe.

To fulfill this function, we can opt for integrated mirror /coat hanger/ drawer solutions, like the one proposed above.

If we are faced with entrances open to other environments, we can opt for less bulky furnishings.

Alternatively, you can choose wall hangers that liven up the environment.

WALL HANGER

To contain the clothes, you can choose to create a built-in wardrobe as in the case of the semi-open entrance, or even choose storage mirrors that, in addition to containing, also give depth to the environment.

INTEGRATED SHELVES AND HANGERS

Finally, to have supports for other types of objects, there are complements that combine the coat hangers with the shelves, which is

a real wall organizer, made by hand with the wooden structure that acts as a container and the sheet metal that is a real wall hanger.

Colors and lights of an entrance

Finally, let's give some advice on colors and lights for an entrance area.

The choice obviously depends very much on the configuration of the space, but in general, light and bright colors are preferred, which give energy and comfort, making those who enter immediately feel at home.

Following the same logic, you should always try to let in as much natural light as you can, but, if this is not possible, it is good to help yourself with the use of artificial lighting systems.

SUSPENSION LAMPS

You can opt for a central light that illuminates the whole space or create an exciting atmosphere by playing with central lighting bodies and wall sconces, switched on alternately or all together.

If you have an entrance with a very high ceiling it is better to choose suspension lamps that come down to illuminate the whole area well, while with low ceilings it is better to opt for ceiling or flush wall lighting.

GROUPED PENDANT LAMPS

Finally, when we are faced with an imposing entrance, play can also be made with grouped lighting bodies, reminiscent of nature with its organic forms.

Ideas and projects

Hallway furniture is a fundamental choice for two reasons: organization and decor. You will find many ideas for a modern entrance online, on Pinterest and on Instagram.

It is said that the entrance is our business card: it is the first space in which guests enter, a preview of your home and the imprint you wanted to give it. Think about it: have you ever presented yourself with an untrimmed beard, mismatched socks, a gym sweatshirt ... to a client, to a job interview or a first date?

I bet not.

Here, in the eyes of a guest, your entrance speaks of you and the way you live in the house.

A tidy entrance reflects your personality and makes you feel better every day after returning from work. Here you can finally shut out stress and tensions.

If you are wondering how to furnish the entrance to your home or apartment, first you need to analyze what type of entrance you have and the space available: only in this way will you be able to understand what you really need. The first tip is: don't get stuck on the classic pre-packaged entrance set, the cabinet with drawer and coat hooks.

Maybe it's just the right one, maybe it's not and you can take advantage of the space with something more intelligent and structured.

WHAT DO YOU NEED IN THE HALL OF THE HOUSE?

Once you have ascertained how much space you have and what type it is (small or large, a wall, two walls, a corner, a niche, an entire room ...)

you need to understand what you need and how you can meet your needs using the right furniture. The options you will have are:

TO CONTAIN

Shoes, coats, umbrellas, dog leash, keys, briefcases, handbags backpacks, sports equipment (for example: skateboard, electric scooter or folding bicycle).

In this case you will need a wardrobe, a coatrack or a real wardrobe, mirror or mirror-container, bench to sit down to put on/take off shoes.

LEARN

In a small entrance, perhaps not divided from the rooms of the living area, there is often only space for hooks and coat hangers. Just what you need for the jackets and the bag you use every day.

In this case you will need wall hangers (equipped panels, hooks, knobs), on the ground or on the ceiling. If the wall and the shape of the room allow it, you can complete the hanging area with a mirror and / or a shelf.

SUPPORT

If at the entrance you just want a space to place your bag, wallet, keys and mail, the solution is simple: opt for a bench, a console, a small hall cupboard or shelves.

TO DECORATE

You have a large house and you need to furnish a large entrance. You have no space problems and therefore you do not need to organize the

entrance making it functional. In this case you can focus only on embellishing this area with sculptural elements, a carpet, armchairs, an entrance table or a large mirror.

HOUSE WITHOUT ENTRANCE

It happens more and more frequently and not only in one-room or two-room apartments. Modern three-room and four-room apartments also often open directly onto the living area. The ideal solution is to make the most of the walls adjacent to the door with what you need most. Remember to think before buying: do you want to contain, hang, place or decorate?

You can also define the walls of this area with a different color or with wallpaper.

Another solution is to create a fifth partition through plasterboard walls or, even better, a double-sided bookcase. If space is at a minimum, even a simple shelf and a few coat hanger knobs hooked to the wall will certainly do a great job. Another useful element can be a pouf on which to sit to remove shoes or to place a bag.

HERE ARE THE MAIN SOLUTIONS FOR A HOUSE WITHOUT A SEPARATE ENTRANCE.

Solution # 1: the coat hanger (on the ground, on the wall, on the ceiling)

Definitely a minimal solution. Free-standing or wall-mounted coat hangers for hanging everyday jackets, scarves and bags. The essential contained in an accessory with a minimum size. Considering that you will always be able to see it, focus on aesthetics with a designer coat hanger. There is something for everyone, even with integrated lighting.

Even a free-standing designer coat hanger can solve many problems, acting both as a coat hanger and as a room divider. On the shelf you can place bags, slippers or shoes.

If the walkable square meters are very limited ... look up! There are ceiling hangers that, in addition to saving you space, are very beautiful to look at.

Even more minimalist solution are coat hooks. Coat hooks offer no standing surfaces, but they do a great job with jackets, bags, scarves. Better if it's decorative since you will always be able to see tham: they will furnish your non-entrance with an original touch.

Even a small coat rack / valet stand can save you from clutter and you can also place it in the hallway or behind the door.

Solution # 2: the mirror

This too, a minimal idea. Choose it with integrated coat hooks to combine two functions in one.

If you don't have space, choose an essential mirror or an intelligent opening or swivel model that turns into a coat hanger when needed.

Solution # 3: the winning trio of mirrors, shelves and coat hangers

With an eye to aesthetics, the trio mirror + shelf + coat hanger is always welcome. On one side jackets and bags, on the other wallets, mail, keys and mirror for one last look at your look, before going out.

Solution # 4: ottoman, bench, chair

Pouf, bench but also a chair with a particular design or a vintage piece: it takes little to embellish an entrance that leads directly into the living area. More beautiful but also more functional, because thanks to a seat you can obtain a corner where you can sit to put on or take off your shoes, a support surface for bags and a backrest on which to hang one or two jackets.

Solution # 5: derive an entrance

A corner you don't know how to use is invaluable when you have little space. Just close it with a structure with doors, or a custom-built wardrobe to obtain a very useful compartment where there was nothing before.

Entrance open to the living room

How to furnish an entrance to the living room? An increasingly widespread formula, now predominant in modern homes, is the open space entrance that opens directly onto the living area. It requires careful consideration of the spaces to be dedicated to the entrance area. It is necessary to create a stylistic harmony between two areas which, despite having a different function, share the same room.

Solution # 1: divide the entrance from the living room

Arrange a piece of furniture or a structure that acts as a "filter" or "fifth" partition. The ideal is a double-sided bookcase with a choice of low models (perfect behind the sofa) or high dividing bookcases also in floor-to-ceiling models (also called "uprights" or "poles").

Double-sided wardrobe

If you have enough space, you can think of creating an entrance separating it from the rest of the living room with a dividing wardrobe. You can choose a very tall model or a standard height one, and equip it with a coat rack and shoe rack.

Solution # 2: make the entrance from the equipped wall or from the bookcase

If you foresee a modular bookcase in the living room, you can use it for books but also as a TV wall unit. You could think of converting a part of it into entrance furniture, after all, a few shelves for bags and objects are enough, or a compartment closed by doors to use as a wardrobe and shoe rack.

Solution # 3: use a sideboard, console table, desk or chest of drawers

If you don't need hangers, opt for a low cabinet that blends in well with the rest of the furniture, such as a particular small sideboard or console table.

Suspended drawers for the entrance can perform an excellent function of containment and support. If they can be combined with each other and integrated with shelves, panels and cabinets, they offer infinite design possibilities.

Entrance with staircase

With the widespread use of the "duplex" formula in newly or recently built apartments, solutions are increasingly required to furnish this area. If the entrance is not delimited but opens directly onto the living room, the advice is to follow the ideas we have given you above for the living room. If, on the other hand, you have a real entrance or lobby, read on.

Entrance under the mezzanine

Very popular in studios and small industrial-style lofts, this solution is not unlike that of the duplex. If used well it helps to obtain extra spaces that are always useful in small one-room apartments, pieds-a-terre and two-roomed lofts. Look at the project: under the mezzanine a separate entrance has been created with the function of coat cupboard and closet. The furniture is easily solved with modular walk-in closet modules.

Duplex with entrance door under the staircase

Here you will need to furnish the wall adjacent to the door: if you have to put the TV wall unit on this same wall, it is advisable to provide an all-encompassing solution that acts as both an entrance and living room furniture. Alternatively, you can use another wall ... obviously everything always depends on the space available!

Entrance on an atrium

We find this kind of configuration in single houses, usually built in the 60s or 70s, where the ground floor is entirely dedicated to accessory rooms. This type of entrance usually also has access to garages and various rooms (storage room, laundry room, cellar, hobby room), with an apartment on the upper floors. In this case the ground floor is a passage area but, even if small, it provides an ideal space to leave shoes, overcoats, work shoes, bicycles, and various equipment.

If you have enough square meters available, you can also think about completely furnishing this area with wardrobes.

Corridor entrance

Typical of the apartments of the 60s and 70s is the long corridor on which the doors that lead to the various rooms of the house open (kitchen, living room, sitting room, dining room, bedrooms or hallway of the sleeping area which in turn leads to the bedroom/ bedrooms, and bathroom). A dedicated area where you can organize yourself perfectly with a real entrance furniture with overcoat, shoe rack and mirror. If the corridor is narrow and long, it is better to use the walls with suspended furniture and with reduced depth. If the width allows it, we can think of more articulated wardrobes in which there is really room for everything.

Even a chest of drawers "stolen" from the bedroom can be a perfect solution for a hallway entrance, or in any case a space separated from the rest of the house, square or rectangular. Just choose an original color or shape, maybe add a mirror, and that's it.

A perfect composition so as not to occupy the floor is that of shelves, containers and wall hangers.

Tiny house? House by the sea or in the mountains? Optimize the entrance hallway with a rollaway bed.

It can be very useful in a studio apartment or in a small two-room apartment where, from time to time, there is the need for an additional bed. A retractable bed that also acts as a support surface for bags, wallets, keys ... but which turns into a comfortable bed for guests in a few seconds. A perfect idea also for those who have to furnish a holiday home.

Entrance directly into the kitchen

If as soon as you open the door you find yourself in the kitchen you can opt for the so-called "bookcase terminal" or for a module closed by a door that you can use to store jackets and bags.

Take advantage of a niche at the entrance

If the depth allows it, the best option is to opt for a custom built-in wardrobe. Inside it is possible to set up a wardrobe, a shoe rack, a closet and even a laundry room.

It may happen that for architectural reasons you find yourself with a niche in the wall that you don't know how to enhance. If it is small or shallow you can fill it with shelves (on the wall or attached to a boiserie on which you can add other elements such as coat hooks or storage bases).

Furnish a large entrance

Square or rectangular, a large entrance poses fewer problems than a small one. For limited spaces it is necessary to strive to find the right piece of furniture and understand what we really need in order not to run into the risk of over-furnishing. But when the house is spacious and has an entrance separate from the rest of the rooms, the task is certainly easier. Just put everything you need into it!

If you also have a garage, or cellar, the entrance loses much of its practical function, leaving you free to put the decor and aesthetics first.

If in the entrance you do not need purely functional furnishings, that's a green light for large mirrors, consoles with a particular design, benches, rugs, bookcases, armchairs or chaises longue and coffee tables.

THE BOISERIE / CONCEALED WARDROBE

A wardrobe that is there but not seen and that, on the contrary, embellishes the environment with a look that recalls that of the wooden paneling of period houses. With full-height doors, shelves or equipped compartments, your entrance is transformed into a functional room, without sacrificing aesthetics.

JAPANESE ENTRANCE

It's called Genkan (玄関) and it's one of our favorites. In fact, it arises from the practice of not stepping on the floor of the house - usually wood and in some cases tatami mats - with shoes, for 3 reasons: not to bring dirt and dust inside; clearly divide the inside from the outside (even on a spiritual level); do not damage the precious tatami made from rice straw. The genkan provides a separate area (tame) usually lower than the real floor of the house, often clearly separated from it by sliding doors (fusuma or shoji depending on the position).

TRADITIONAL SCANDINAVIAN ENTRANCE

In northern Europe it is customary to have a separate entrance for obvious reasons related to the climate. Outside, the temperature can be extreme, so tradition provides for an access door to a small atrium, sometimes equipped with a small bathroom, anteroom or closet in which to leave shoes and coats wet from snow and rain. Current trends are more stylish, but there is often the wall wardrobe (or a well-equipped niche with shelves and hooks) and the tactical hangers placed near the radiator.

ENGLISH COUNTRY ENTRANCE (THE MUDROOM)

Moving into the Anglo-Saxon world, the English entrance to traditional homes includes a mudroom. As for the rest of the Nordic world, it is a small room or an entrance corridor where, as the name reveals, you leave clothes, shoes and galoshes, the beloved wellies dripping with rain and mud at the end of a walk on the foggy moors.

Why did we choose these ideas from the world? There is one thing that unites them and that we believe is fundamental: take off your shoes and leave them at the entrance! An excellent practice for a cleaner home, for hygiene, for comfort at home and for the protection of floors (especially parquet).

Do you want to copy these solutions? For the oriental entrance you can decide to create a space at the entrance covered with a different floor, perhaps more resistant and washable. For the Nordic style, opt for benches, baskets or chests in which to leave shoes and coats. If space and budget allow you, you can create a separate area with plasterboard walls or custom built-in wardrobes.

Best practice: 5 tips for an orderly (and beautiful) entrance

- We will never tire of repeating it: do not leave your shoes on the floor at the entrance. The solutions, you have seen, are many, from the most banal shoe cabinet to small wardrobes or sideboards to be converted into shoe racks. The important thing is not to leave them around because they immediately convey a feeling of disorder.

- Immediately up or put away coats, jackets, hats, scarves in their place. Do not leave them randomly placed on chairs or on the armrests of the sofa. If you do not have space at the entrance, provide hooks in another part of the house or a space inside the wardrobe in the room dedicated to "outdoor" clothing.

- Prepare a space for keys, wallets, documents, envelopes etc ... a box, a tray, a drawer, hooks

  bags, backpacks, laptop cases: if you have a small entrance, try to keep only one of these, the one you use every day. Avoid leaving your gym, swimming pool or soccer bag in sight. You can hang them on hooks, place them on a bench or ottoman, put them in a basket. If you have more space then put them inside a specially equipped wardrobe or on shelves.

- a small decorative carpet at the entrance is always a good idea: it is beautiful, it is soft and welcoming, it protects the floor, it traps the dust that enters the door or that we carry under our shoes.

You can stop here to take off your shoes, avoiding bringing residues of earth and pebbles into the house. You can use it to place your shopping bags on them as you enter or to safely take off your wet raincoat without spilling drops onto the floor. It is the ideal space to help children take off their shoes or booties and put on their slippers, or even to let your 4-legged friend sit while you dry him after a walk in the rain. There's nothing a good carpet cleaner and a spin in the washing machine can't get rid of, and the floor is safe!

How to organize it and make the most of it

The entrance to an apartment appears, when it is messy, to be not thought of, arranged haphazardly!

The entrance to an apartment, in addition to giving the first impression of you and your hearth, is also an area that needs to be functional and not neglected.

Very often at the entrance there is an unsightly electrical panel that needs to be covered, but always accessible.

The furniture for the entrance of the house is one of the most difficult environments to design for an architect, but it is also stimulating because most of the time it requires tailor-made solutions.

What to put at the entrance so that it is not too anonymous?

How to furnish the small or narrow entrance?

Better coat hangers, or shelves?

How to illuminate the entrance if it is dark or blind?

What mistakes to avoid?

These are some of the most heinous doubts that haunt this particular space. But let's see them in detail.

What to put at the entrance so that it is not too anonymous?

An entrance must first express a character.

To do this it must have two key elements:

- The right light

- A thoughtful "lightness".

There is nothing worse than entering an apartment and being immediately suffocated by distorted furniture, perhaps disproportionate to the context and even too illuminated with showroom spotlights.

Remember that you are at home and it is not necessary to deploy all the LED lights you can find.

The entrance to the house must be light and elegant and must announce what will later be seen in the rest of the house.

Said with a metaphor, it's like a movie trailer. Suggest without revealing.

There is no point in changing the style or over-decorating it like a Christmas tree. Instead, it must be a crescendo overture, until you enter the living area.

Mistakes to avoid

You must avoid making the following mistakes like the plague:

- Overdosing on the colors, generating a 90's pizzeria effect

- Go overboard with the lights. Follow these rules to illuminate the entrance.

- Go overboard with the furnishings

- Don't take into account the real spaces available

- Don't make it functional

- Do not insert any furniture that is also a container

- Using a style that is too different from the rest of the house.

I would distinguish between small entrances and large entrances.

The small ones are obviously the most problematic.

When designing the division of an interior, it is a good idea to make sure that the entrance has a source of natural light and that it is not infested with doors leading elsewhere.

In fact, an entrance with too many doors can easily disorient and leave a negative perception to those who enter.

If you have a spacious and bright house, you can furnish the entrance with a sculpture, which makes it more minimalist and refined.

Furnishing a small entrance

When an entrance is very small, perhaps like a corridor or even less, it is useless to get stuck with the furniture. The furniture would clutter up the space further, to the detriment of its organization.

In small rooms, avoid clutter and simply use a small console table and a mirror. They should be more than enough.

If you need a hanger, you can add visible elements, such as small nails to match the wall, to be kept very organized to minimize the chaos effect.

This also applies if you have an entrance with a staircase that leads you elsewhere.

Clever use of wall mirrors allows you to broaden the perception of space and make the entrance seem larger.

How to furnish the entrance to an open space house

The open space entrance projects you immediately inside the house, usually in the living area or kitchen.

In this case, since you have more space, you can think of inserting a wardrobe or overcoat, built into the wall, to make the space more minimal and tidier.

You don't have to do much else, just go along with the decor of the room you enter and don't overdo the decorations.

Everything must seem natural and simple, making sure to direct the attention of those who enter towards the center of the house, which can be the sofa or the kitchen.

How to enhance the entrance to the house

The secrets to making an entrance bigger are:

Use full height mirrors. They manage to give an unparalleled sense of depth.

Work on colors, preferring light ones.

Decorate with horizontal stripes or bands, which increase the perception of space.

Pay attention to the light, which can make a space smaller.

Look for a "wow" element that draws visual attention.

Better a coat hanger or a shelf?

In theory, a coat hanger is more useful. I prefer, when possible, to build it into the wall so as not to make the sides of the piece of furniture too evident and to maintain an elegant, minimalist design.

This allows you to hide bags, jackets, umbrellas and much more, so I find it more practical. Read also how to hide air conditioners, radiators and roller shutter boxes.

If space does not allow, it is better to use a console or a shelf that empties pockets.

At least you will have a place to store the keys and not scatter them around the house.

Choose a shelf with a drawer to place a clipboard, spare keys, emergency flashlight, a small portable sewing kit and anything else you need to find right away.

How to light up a dark or blind entrance

Obviously, an entrance with natural light has a completely different impact than a dark or blind one, so open space or window solutions are preferred.

If this is not possible, you must design the light like this:

- lighting from above, with spotlights or, better, LED luminous cuts in the ceiling. Avoid the central suspensions because they could be annoying when passing through or when opening the door.

- décor lighting, with lighting effects that decorate. If the entrance is small, it can be a solution to give a "wow" effect with little. If it is not necessary, leave this point alone.

- illumination that is not seen. Hide led bars or lights behind cuts, furniture, cabinets, to make sure that the light comes out without showing the lamp.

LIVING ROOM

---

10 things that cannot be missing in a modern living room

Do you know what are the 10 things that cannot be missing in a modern living room? Surely it is easy to guess the TV and the sofa, but be careful because these too must have very specific characteristics and then there is much more. If you are curious, here are all the details!

This trend, in fact, has very specific characteristics that must be respected if an optimal result is to be obtained. For example, natural materials are preferred, furniture with very clean lines and a lot of attention is paid to the accessories and ornaments.

Let's see together then what are 10 things that cannot be missing in a modern living room.

1. Corner sofa

2. Tv

3. Low design coffee table

4. Bookcase

5. Carpet

6. Lamps

7. Minimal equipped wall

8. Mirror

9. Art

10. Plants

1. Corner sofa

In a modern living room the protagonist is the sofa. This has clean lines and has a very simple structure. A corner model, if the size of the room allows it, cannot be missing.

In fact, it is wider and more comfortable, ideal for accommodating more people or simply for relaxing by stretching out your legs. In short, after a long day this is just what you need, so don't hesitate to choose a corner sofa for the modern living room.

2. Tv

Modern style goes hand in hand with technology and consequently electronic appliances cannot be missing when furnishing according to this trend.

In fact, these are not just accessories, but they become one of the characteristics that distinguish the modern room. For this, there must absolutely be a TV in the living room. Ultra-thin screen models are in fashion.

3. Low design coffee table

When furnishing according to the modern style, clean lines are always preferred. This, however, does not mean that we must stop at furnishings with rectangular or square shapes. On the contrary, instead, objects with a particular design are also sought after, capable of attracting attention.

For example, a low table with particular shapes cannot be missing in the modern living room. Look for something unique, capable of beautifying the environment.

4. Bookcase

In the modern living room, the bookcase is always present. This can also occupy an entire wall and be made to measure, for example with plasterboard.

Generally, the modern bookcase has particular shapes, it can be in wood, but also in metal, it depends on the colors you have chosen for your living room.

5. Carpet

The carpet is never missing in the living room. Generally, it is placed at the foot of the sofa or under the low table. In a modern living room, where neutral colors predominate, it is essential to give a little three-dimensionality.

The dimensions must be chosen in proportion to the size of the room. For example, if the living room is small, you shouldn't choose a carpet that is too big and it shouldn't have too strong colors.

6. Lamps

When decorating in a modern style, you need to pay close attention to lighting. In fact, it is essential that light is spread evenly inside the room.

For this, there is also a need for lamps in addition to the central chandelier. In these cases, designer floor lamps to put next to the sofa cannot be missing.

7. Minimal equipped wall

In every self-respecting living room, an equipped wall cannot be missing. Today, however, it has become much more minimal. For example, very often we opt for suspended cabinets.

Another perfect alternative for modern living is also to simply mount a few shelves next to the TV. They can be at the same height or on several levels.

8. Mirror

Mirrors are often placed in the hall or in the bedroom, but not always in the living room. In reality, putting them also in the living room could be very advantageous.

First, they reflect light and then the room will seem even brighter. Then, they'll also make it look bigger for an optical illusion. In short, a mirror cannot be missing in a modern living room.

9. Art

When decorating the living room, you must never forget to embellish the walls. To do this, pictures can be hung. But be careful, because these too must be in line with the style of furniture you have chosen.

For this reason, in a modern living room, paintings with abstract lines and shapes must be chosen, with bright shades so that they can add a little color to the environment.

10. Plants

The modern style pays a lot of attention to the environment and tries to be closer and closer to nature. For this reason, a green touch with plants cannot be missing in a modern living room.

Among other things, these are perfect for embellishing the room or even for filling some slightly emptier corner. Smaller plants can also be placed on some furniture as if they were an ornament.

Living room wall color: 5 paint combinations for a makeover

Deciding on the best color to paint the living room walls with can be as challenging as the whole house.

This is because it is the only room that catches the eyes of all friends and family, as it is the social space where you entertain with guests.

When it comes to looking for living room color ideas you need to keep two points in mind:

1. Choose a shade that you like and the right contrast that will leave guests pleasantly surprised every time they enter the room;

2. Choose colors that can help increase the size of the space, making it more comfortable and inviting.

Choose the color of the living room walls

If you need to change your living room color, here are some palette combinations to try, which will be very trendy in the coming years. The choice of one rather than another depends on the style of your furniture, on the size of the space (and at the same time on the light that characterizes it), on your desire to dare and on the final mood you want to create.

Let's get to the heart of it!

Palette 1: Dust Blue, Gray and Yellow

You can bring a refreshing touch to your living room by adding a rich dusty blue hue to the current mix.

Generally, this palette is recommended when you have bleached parquet, gray or fairly soft colors on the floor.

Naturally the powder blue (a mix between blue and gray) must be well dosed, in the sense that, depending on the light that characterizes the space, you can decide whether to paint a large or medium wall or two at most.

Make sure that the painted wall is the accent wall, which is where you placed the sofa or TV.

You can also incorporate shades of acid green or yellow via living room accessories like pillows, rugs, and decorative items.

If the sofa is gray, this look amplifies its Spartan appeal through a range of scattered shades of gray to create a comfortable take on warm minimalism. The furnishings should not be too flashy, with dull woods or more or less dark neutral colors.

The partial blue background behind the TV is an inspiring element, full of energy and character.

Palette 2: Dark Gray, Sage Green and Caramel

The combination of dark gray and caramel could be one of the happiest combinations for the living room, as it has the ability to make the room darker and gives character.

Ideal for those who love welcoming spaces and want to break away from a previously clear situation, for example.

Add shades of dove gray, black or white furniture and accessories to create a moody and comforting warmth.

This combination is very effective if you have oak floors and furniture that is not too heavy.

Palette 3: Light Grays and Textures

An easy way to transform the look of your living room without changing all the furnishings is to decorate it with interesting fabrics via colorful rugs, blankets, pillows, paintings and more.

The rest can remain completely neutral, with a prevalence of grays and whites.

Make sure that when you select a prominent fabric like a carpet or drapery, it is in accordance with the overall look and color scheme of your design. Opt for pieces that have an unusual and interesting print.

In this way the fabric design will create a unique (accent) element in your room and make it appear more personalized and cared for. You can also enhance the look of your living room by placing a particular plaid on a sofa or chair.

Since there are a lot of grays, make sure there is wood, such as parquet or warm furniture.

Palette 4: Neutrals always current

Neutrals never go out of fashion. When you want to create a look that lasts for a long time, choose a very simple and bright palette. On the other hand, the neutral house may lack that "wow" touch that other colors can provide.

The neutral color, which is not necessarily white, brings infinite tranquility and well-being, in situations where the living room is a peaceful refuge after work and with friends.

In this case the gaze always falls on the connected spaces. Connected spaces will likely all receive the same color treatment, leaving a large window or light cut in evidence.

The neutral on the walls is an "easy way" to furnish. The important thing is to know how to create a minimum of contrast so as not to fall into the banal.

Palette 5: Brown and orange

When you have a dark floor, don't overdo it with color or other dark walls.

I like to keep myself in a neutral mood with a few touches of orange or green or blue in rugs, cushions, chairs and other accessories. This is to ensure that the floor is a protagonist without mixing with the rest.

Leave a lot of white on the walls and, if necessary, work on a single wall, with a color or with a large painting.

If you have two prima donnas at home, it's hard to get them to cooperate. Better to bring out one of the two and give the other a fundamental role in assisting the accent. I know, it sounds Arabic, but that's it!

When you're designing a room, it's really cool to think about the future, what it will look like. When you imagine the spaces in your home, it is good to think about a certain common thread of colors from one room to another. While each room has its own unique design, you must always be aware of how it will tie into adjacent spaces and within the palette of the entire home.

What to put behind the sofa: the 24 most beautiful ideas to copy

Start from space

No performance anxiety

Decorate the wall behind the sofa with paintings

A small buffet table

Bookcases and tall elements

Have you bought the sofa in your new living room and are in crisis because you don't know what to put behind the sofa?

I know, it happens very often, as well as to match and arrange the sofas in the living room.

The attitudes for furnishing the wall behind the sofa are essentially two:

- fear of too much emptiness

- fear of overflow.

In any case, fear of making mistakes.

In this chapter I want to give you some suggestions on what to put behind the sofa and finally complete the living room without getting panic attacks or ending up arguing with your life partner.

Start from the space

Exactly! Which does not mean taking a one-way trip to the moon, it means considering the real square footage available to you and whether the sofa needs space on the sides or at the back.

In this case the situation changes.

You can't overcrowd a living room where the sofa is in front of a window.

Same story if you have a passage behind it because it is located in the middle of the room.

Take it easy, as the Eagles said in 1977, take it easy. First study your context well.

- large paintings behind the sofa
- living room with pictures behind, the sofa in front

No performance anxiety

I'll tell you something that will perhaps upset your way of seeing the living room:

Often, putting nothing (or almost nothing) behind the sofa is better than filling it with meaningless furniture or decorations.

An interior that has not been studied is synonymous with poor design vision, that is to say that in a certain sense you do not know how to be an interior designer (and it is a good thing, all in all!).

As I often say: when in doubt, choose elegance. Or at least, never use things you aren't sure about.

A wood or plaster boiserie, a wallpaper or a simple void give much more importance to the sofa than many trinkets placed everywhere or, worse, paintings taken from everywhere and placed without a style or a visual hierarchy.

In this case, it seems obvious, the sofa must have unparalleled style and importance.

So, I'm not talking about the sofa taken from the furniture market, or the leather-like massage chairs.

Those are the anti-design par excellence!

Instead, I'm talking about a large sofa, perhaps with a chaise longue, soft, with a precious fabric or sinuous shapes.

In short, something of quality.

In this case it is permissible to be minimalist.

Decorate the wall behind the sofa with paintings.

If you have an interior in Scandinavian or contemporary style, or even classic-contemporary, you can be daring with a figurative wall.

Ok to paintings, but be careful!

The arrangement must be treated in detail.

You can opt for a shelf on which to place the frames and change them at will during the year without having to puncture the wall, or for a "hanging" arrangement, with paintings all the same or in black and white or monochromatic.

Hang the photos of the beach with the family, of the children in kindergarten or of a couple's vacation in Japan while eating miso.

Just because there would be so many colors to manage in the photographs that the minestrone effect is just around the corner.

How to decorate the wall behind the sofa with paintings

Here, too, a minimalist approach is the solution.

A few elements, but essential.

How to decorate the wall behind the sofa with essential paintings

Needless to say, the paintings must match something in the room.

With an armchair, cushions, a carpet or the color of the furniture.

A small buffet table

If the sofa is in the center of the room, you can build a small low cabinet, also called a buffet, to place things on, like books, or simply to act as a shoulder and not show off the back of the sofa (which is not always beautiful).

This solution is functional even if the living room is in an open space with the kitchen.

It would also be advisable to have a very thin plasterboard or wooden partition created (no more than 15cm thick) to act as a shoulder and to place small design objects or a led strip with lights directed towards the ceiling.

Bookcases and tall elements

In stately homes or with large spaces, you often see the sofa very close to a bookcase or a wall container.

I find this an elegant and luxury solution, ideal if you want to give your house an edge.

To have a top look it is necessary that these storage units are made of precious woods, metals or with an ethnic or particular design, also combined with mirrors.

If, on the other hand, your interior is smaller and less pretentious, you can opt for a wall mirror or one placed on the ground, moving the sofa further forward.

For many architects the mirror is out of fashion, I find it a simple and always effective stratagem to expand the space.

How to choose the right carpet: models, size, color combinations

Carpet - yes or no?

- Which carpet to choose?

- How big should the carpet be?

- Tips for choosing the carpet for the living room

- Ideas for choosing the right carpet

- How to match the carpet to the furniture

- Palette carpet

- Scenic carpet

- Minimalist carpet

Choosing the carpet to place in the living room or bedroom is one of the most frequent doubts when it comes to furnishing the house in its final touches.

In fact, there are a myriad of materials, colors, shapes, and compositions.

Choose the carpet

Before seeing some design pieces in detail, it is necessary to make a couple of small premises.

Carpet - yes or no?

The carpet is a complement that furnishes a lot. Not all homes need a carpet and not all carpets can be placed everywhere. Today it is possible to choose between different shapes and sizes, creating even very special combinations that greatly enhance the living room, bathroom and bedroom.

Which carpet to choose?

A carpet is a fairly expensive piece of furniture. Many are laboriously hand-knotted to allow for a great deal of detail and a soft finish. I advise you to choose the quality, being difficult to machine wash, so it could accumulate a lot of dust and dirt over the years. Materials of dubious strength / origin will create significantly less hygienic environments.

Choose a short-haired model if you want something more practical and manageable directly with the vacuum cleaner.

How big should the carpet be?

Even the carpet can be sized and proportioned to the furniture. Indeed, it must!

Depending on the size of the sofa, it is a good idea to choose one of these layouts shown in the figure, with a "different size". A good rule of thumb is to make sure that at least 2 of the 4 sofa legs rest on the carpet, in order to cover the foot band of the seated person.

How to place the carpet in front of the sofa

In the case of a carpet for the bedroom, here too you can choose between different sizes. The important thing is that the area on which you rest your feet is covered once you get out of bed.

How to place the carpet in the bedroom

Choose the carpet, remember not to lay the carpets near the doors so as not to obstruct the passage too much and always size them in proportion to the room. Any table must be placed on top. If there is more than one coffee table, at least one of them must be on top of the carpet.

They are definitely the decors that last the longest in terms of time and overall style.

A little more inflated today are the Persian carpets, already seen and full of colors, such as to create a certain chromatic confusion, especially when it comes to carpets in shades of red, burgundy or orange.

Let's say that it would be better to use them with colder and duller colors (gray, blue, ...) or with classical furnishings.

The choice of carpet depends a lot on the room it is placed in and the overall look of the room. A rug that you will have to put in the bathroom will not be the same size or the same design as one in the dining room.

The new proposals of the brands are mostly geometric or a little eccentric.

Here, the carpet can furnish or simply complete a look: you decide how much it should be the protagonist in the room.

Indoor rugs can be considered as real works of art. If they are not plain colored pieces, they should be chosen in the same way as a painting. Indeed, sometimes rugs can really replace paintings and can be fixed to the walls, vertically. Or even on the stairs, creating an exceptional effect.

These are very evidently decorative pieces, which create environments with a strong aesthetic impact.

Before choosing the carpet, I always recommend investing in a certain design: the carpet is a piece of furniture that needs dedicated styling because it must communicate effectively with the floor, the sofa and the rest of the environment.

Another viable idea is to insert several rugs close together. You can choose between different shapes or use the same shape, for example two circles or a circle and another, irregular, shape.

It goes without saying that the two rugs together should communicate: it could be the same rug of different sizes, or two rugs with similar palettes, or even the same rug with complementary colors.

Let yourself be carried away by your imagination!

How to match the carpet to the furniture

Do you want to choose the carpet without making a mistake?

There are several strategies to insert the right carpet into the environment. Let's see some of them:

Palette carpet

If you want to create a soft environment, look for a rug that matches the same tones as the room. Possibly in plain color or slightly decorated, in order to create a simple and relaxing tone.

Poliform carpet

Generally, it is good to create a certain gap between the floor and the sofa, which you can facilitate with a nice rug. For example, if the floor is medium parquet and the sofa is gray, you can choose an ecru-colored rug to create the right contrast between the two elements.

Scenic carpet

The carpet can also be disruptive and intentionally grab attention. Look for a beautiful and refined motif, with a color outside the palette chosen for the home, in such a way as to make that portion of the room the protagonist as if it were a point underlined with a highlighter.

It must be a thoughtful choice, never casual. The house will take on a more eclectic attitude which can break the monotony. If you have, for example, a gray floor and a gray sofa, a colored rug is a good opportunity to break the monotony and make the space more interesting.

Minimalist carpet

When you already have different colors in the room or a wallpaper, it is good not to overdo the decoration on the carpet. It all depends on

where you want to put the accent in the room. Theoretically, if you have patterned wallpaper, you shouldn't go overboard with other decorations!

Choose a minimalist one-color or two-tone rug that adds uniqueness and personality to any residential or contract space, visually increasing the feeling of calm, fluidity and comfort.

The curved carpet softens the shapes of a small, rectangular or too rigid environment.

Choose the most suitable carpet for your home and create a dream look!

How to furnish a rectangular living room in 4 steps

How to furnish a rectangular living room?

- Step 1: Find the longest opaque wall in the room
- Step 2: Don't be anxious to fill all the walls
- Step 3: Always keep the flow and steps in mind
- Step 4: Divide the space (ideally)
- Step 5: Pay attention to the color palette

The two secrets of the architect for furnishing a rectangular living room:

- Maximize vertical space
- Break the monotony with a wow effect

Are you struggling with a small or large rectangular living room, but you have no idea how to furnish it to create an elegant environment or at least not to make it appear too monotonous?

If you don't know how to develop the full potential of a rectangular (or square) living room, these tips of mine will probably be useful to you.

In this chapter I would like to suggest 5 moves to furnish a modern rectangular living room in an elegant way, even if it has nothing particular about the shape.

These are simple but always effective tips, which I also use in my rectangular living room projects.

Warning: the distribution of a rectangular room always depends on the number of doors and windows it houses and their position.

Living rooms with many windows certainly don't scare me, on the contrary, it means that the living room will be bright, which is always an added value.

The caveat is that the rectangular living room ideas proposed here will certainly vary from house to house, depending on the size or, indeed, the number of openings.

I realize that organizing a rather large space can sometimes be difficult for the layman.

Here I'll come to your aid!

Step 1: Find the longest opaque wall in the room

Exactly. Easy, right?

Good. In this windowless wall or section of wall you will need to place the television and / or fireplace or other accent elements.

It will be important to focus visual attention and not to lose the eye in too many directions.

Depending on the size of the room, rectangular living rooms often have more than one accent focal point.

Architectural features such as a fireplace, wallpaper, or large panoramic window are integrated focal points.

A large wall-mounted television, a designer display cabinet, a large wall art painting, or a piano could serve as a second focal point.

Step 2: Don't be anxious to fill all the walls

As I have already explained in this post, you do not necessarily have to place all the furniture "stuck" to the long and short walls. If you have the right space, it's nice to insert a sofa in the center of the room or a particular divider.

Furniture pushed against a wall in a narrow living room emphasizes the length of the space. Instead, moving a piece of furniture away from the walls will allow you to create a cozy seating area without necessarily having a void in the center.

Step 3: Always keep the flow and steps in mind

The architect's design always starts from here.

Create a path for the flow of walkways that is fairly straightforward. The goal is to create an intimate atmosphere instead of an uncomfortable slalom course, dodging too much furniture.

This does not mean that the passage must necessarily be in a straight line!

It could certainly be curved, but it should not force the person to follow a too long and convoluted path to get from one room to another.

Placing a sofa in the middle of the room will create a small seating area with a clear path behind the seat.

If you were able to walk behind the sofa instead of in front, interrupting the TV viewing, it would be better.

The main steps that should coincide with the path of the flow lines on the floor plan require a minimum of 90cm.

A walkway between two pieces of furniture should measure at least 75 cm. Leave 45 cm between the coffee table and the sofa or 30 cm between the coffee table and an armchair.

If your rectangular living room is particularly long, divide it into two separate areas.

The arrangement of the furniture can play an important role in defining the space.

For example, two different conversation areas, or a sitting area and a small office or dining room are options to make the most of the voids.

Use rugs and countertops to better define each area. The priority is to keep the two spaces always tidy and clearly legible.

Step 4: Pay attention to the color palette

Monochromatic and neutral colors bring about a sense of calm in a small or shared setting, though that doesn't mean you always have to settle for the usual color.

White walls and ceiling, with a single accent wall of a different color end up joining and expanding the room.

In the living room it is always better to use a few decorative elements, but of large dimensions.

Opt for one or two giant canvas paintings to break the monotony of a very long wall and create more visual interest.

Conversely, numerous small pictures placed on a wall can create a disheveled and crowded look. Hang a large mirror on a short wall to expand visual perception.

Define and separate functional areas by placing a rug under each arrangement.

A large indoor potted plant can fill a lonely corner while a designer chandelier or floor lamp can help visually divide a long, narrow room with sparkling lighting.

Maximize vertical space

Direct your eye upwards making the most of the vertical space. A full-height wardrobe or bookcase breaks up a space that is too horizontal.

Built-in furniture or full-height shelves are your friends.

They can be used on short walls to add storage space and will inevitably shorten the room.

Especially if one of the longer walls has a focal point, the window wall will grab your attention before the shelving unit.

Break the monotony with a wow effect

If your living room is too flat or uninteresting, you can always break the monotony with a "wow element", for example a bio-fireplace, wallpaper, special lights or a precious covering.

The trick is to distract the attention from the less chic parts to divert it to a prettier and more engaging side. However, this does not mean overdoing it. Always keep the elegance of the shapes to create a dream rectangular living room.

How to furnish a long and narrow living room

Rule # 1: Divide the space

Rule # 2: Create dynamism

Rule 3: Proportion

How to furnish a long and narrow living room? Perhaps it is one of the most difficult steps for those who approach the design of their home.

Sometimes the architectural forms do not help and we find ourselves facing complicated furnishing problems and situations.

Putting all the furniture on the perimeter is not a good strategy!

First of all, don't panic and don't try to place the furniture all around the perimeter of the room!

It is a common attitude that, however, will not lead you to recover more space, on the contrary.

Positioning the furniture on the perimeter, leaving the void in the center, only contributes to giving a sense of NOT having designed your interior. The resulting dimensional jagging of objects creates a visual disorder that is scarcely improvable.

For example, imagine placing the sofa (low), the sideboard (medium height) and a display cabinet or equipped column (high) on the same wall.

The diagonality (worse if pyramidal) that you have created would be a considerable aesthetic disaster!

So, let's see what are the 3 fundamental rules to approach a furniture of this type without making mistakes!

Rule # 1: Divide the space

This does not mean building a wall in the center to permanently divide it!

Instead, it means giving two or more different functions to the space and visually dividing them according to an idea.

For example, in your living room you could create a relaxation area with sofas and a guest dining area with a nice long table and comfortable chairs. Or divide the entrance area from the actual living room.

Or again, as in this project of mine, you can create a small transparent home office to recover unused space and create a bright and multifunctional corner.

Basically, the technique is to ideally divide the space to maintain a better functional order.

It is also possible to divide the space with just the furniture.

Do not place sofas and tables in the same direction! Try to arrange them in such a way as to intersperse horizontal and vertical lines and give more harmony to the overall environment.

I know it's mostly an expert talk, but having a row of furniture one after the other is not nice.

How to place furniture in a long, narrow living room

First of all, decide what the focal point of your room will be. It should theoretically be on the longest wall.

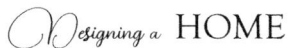
As a general rule it is more correct to insert the TV in the longest closed wall available. This is because the equipped wall is the protagonist of the living room and must be enhanced with the necessary precautions.

I often see huge living rooms that have the TV relegated to a corner or on a narrow wall between two windows.

WRONG!

The TV must be proportional to the size of the living room. And above all, never positioned between two close windows.

How to arrange the sofas in a long and narrow living room?

The sofa, on the other hand, must be placed immediately in front of the equipped wall. It is not good to put the sofas perpendicular to the TV or on one side, or off-center.

It means that the space has not been studied and prepared correctly.

If the room is very large, you can provide a double-sided sofa in the center of the room.

I love this type of upholstery because it allows you to arrange two functions on opposite sides and enjoy two spaces with a single sofa.

For example, you can have the TV on wall A, the double-sided sofa in the middle of the room and a fireplace on wall B, opposite to A.

Double-sided sofas are an ultra-modern system for large enough spaces that help create an interesting and never predictable layout. Read also how to furnish a rectangular living room.

Another trick is to use a sofa with a low or flattened back. In addition to being more contemporary, it helps to maintain an extended perception of space and not to create limits or visual barriers in the living area. It would be a crime to have a sofa with a headrest in the middle of the

room in a large space! The look would be that of a massage sofa in a shopping mall!

Another trick is to use a sectional sofa. Since the backrests are separate pieces from the seats, the entire sofa can be reconfigured a thousand ways to adapt to the situation.

Rule # 2: Create dynamism

Giving an elegant and deluxe look to a living room is not difficult: just keep a discreet and linear approach.

What does it mean? It means that there is no need to overdo it to furnish a long and narrow living room. Start with the larger furniture, sofas, tables, equipped walls, and then continue with the smaller ones, lights and accessories.

How to furnish a long and narrow living room? Small tip: just say "no" to too much furniture.

Instead of having a table with 8 chairs, unused for 90% of the year, choose a smaller table and extra foldable chairs, or poufs to use as seats when needed.

Also considers the flows, i.e. the passages between one area and another and the presence of doors or windows.

It is not easy to generalize especially for this reason, because each space has its starting configuration, but in general, try to keep flows open, without hindering the main passages.

Dynamism can also be created by painting the walls in a correct way.

Rule 3: Proportion

This tip depends on the actual size of your living room.

If you have a large living room with a vaulted ceiling, you definitely don't need to furnish it with a small sofa.

On the flip side, if you live in a studio apartment, a heavy storage wall won't work in your favor. A good rule of thumb for smaller spaces is to look for an apartment-sized sofa or a simple two-seater paired with an easy chair. Modular sofas are the most versatile.

Chairs or ottomans can be moved around easily and have greater flexibility in tight spaces.

The sizing of the carpet is also important to create a harmonious living room. If too small it ends up floating in the room, if too big it seems to have invaded the space!

Choosing a large rug is a trick that makes a room seem larger. Unlike smaller rugs, large sizes do not visually interrupt the floor. The carpet must occupy at least the entire space of the sofa and even go a little further.

Do not overdo the size of the dining table: choose an extendable solution to furnish without crowding.

If there is enough space you can add a sideboard or a buffet as a support surface: even a small desk can be useful for family technological needs.

THE BEDROOM

How to furnish a modern bedroom: 38 trendy ideas

If you are looking for help on how to furnish a modern bedroom, because it lacks personality or because the time has come to renovate it, here you will find my tips and lots of original ideas to copy.

The bedroom is the most intimate room in the house. It says a lot about you, reveals how you are and what you like, without necessarily having to show off.

We focus on the walk-in closet, we struggle to create the right space to put all the things in order, we buy the bed... and then?

Panic.

The husband suggests: - Come on, let's go to the store and look for wallpaper for behind the TV.

The wife mutters: - Okay, but the bedside tables?

The friend: - I saw a beautiful vanity on Instagram, I'm sending you the link!

The mother-in-law: - You should match the colors to the duvet I gave you for Christmas.

The sister: - You can't not put the copper effect lamps on the bedside tables!

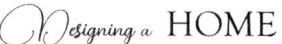

The colleague from the office: - I read in the magazine that dark blue walls are in fashion. Even sage green ones. Even a kind of salmon pink ...

What to do? In the throes of existential crises, maybe you do nothing, or postpone to a later date.

I have seen rooms without bedside tables for more than 6 years, with lamps resting on the floor, TV cables dangling, chairs taken from Ikea on which anything is thrown, shower-like curtains in front of the window hanging from an oblique rod, waiting for more than a "piece of advice", a real miracle.

Yet it takes little, very little to furnish a modern bedroom with these 5 pairs of colors that always work.

There is only one essential element for your bedroom design: the right idea.

A mood that you like is enough to put all the pieces in order, to define a style, a way of being and living in your home.

But let's start with order.

Let's first look at the most important element of the room: drum roll... his Majesty the Bed.

Choosing a double bed or a French bed is completely personal. An architect can give advice, set a style, look for inspiration, but most of the time the client will overturn his choices and buy a bed that he likes.

It is right that this is the case, after all it is not the architect who has to sleep in it.

The bed can be high, low, quilted, simple, in wood, in wrought iron, round, in fabric or even without a headboard.

It matters little.

In general, all beds are adaptable and can fit in an interior (as long as they are not too inlaid or of impractical colors).

What matters is that the bed is "dressed" well.

Exactly.

The structure is secondary because the visual part of the bed is 80% given by the blankets, sheets, and pillows.

So pay close attention to how you dress the bed.

Choose duvets and blankets so you don't have to betray the essence of your room.

Today the most popular look is the soft one, which means lots of pillows, and blankets placed sideways that give an air of being lived in.

Beds that are too rigid are typical of high-ranking hotels, they do not belong in houses.

Of course, if you have an orange duvet and your bedroom is minimalist in oak, that's a big deal.

In this case, instead of throwing everything away to start from scratch (it is always good to be sustainable with our homes), buy or have a duvet cover made in the color you like best, so you can cover up the flaws with style.

Also if you have an important bed frame that you want to disguise, insert a puff cover in linen gauze: cheap and efficient.

How to choose the head of the bed

This is indeed a constant occasion for utter panic.

Decorated?

With paint?

With paintings?

Photo?

With lights, spotlights, LEDs?

Wallpaper?

There are millions of possibilities to furnish a modern bedroom with style.

Here, too, personal taste is king, but there are some small rules to follow.

If the head of the bed is already high, don't add too many elements to your room.

If the bed is not in front of the entrance door, so it is not part of the initial visual impact, you can choose a simpler solution, even just with lights.

If you have already decorated the wall with paint or paper, do not overlap bulky elements (e.g. paintings, furniture or shelves) because you will no longer see the original effect.

If you like wallpaper, don't look for very complex motifs. Make the atmosphere enveloping with warm and relaxing tones. Here you can find 3 of my secrets for choosing wallpaper.

Never forget the color palette. It applies to any room and is a simple guide to making no mistakes.

It is the use of space that suggests the winning solution. Don't look for hyper-decorations, choose elegant simplicity.

The best light is always the natural one. Look for fixtures with a slim profile but with a high level of performance.

Bedroom lighting

Which lights to choose?

This is another top topic.

Lighting a bedroom well is important for two factors: it promotes relaxation and avoids the "hospital room" effect.

The light must be of two types:

Atmospheric (therefore with LEDs or lamps that are never direct or too strong) to use when watching TV, reading a book or simply wanting to rest for a moment. This light must be as indirect as possible, warm and preferably adjustable (dimmable). No too white or cold lights.

Generall never with exposed light bulbs, or with open and dangling central chandeliers without a function, a bit like our grandmothers' bedrooms were.

Today mixed lighting is used: LEDs hidden in the headboard or near the wardrobe; suspended on the bedside tables; with floor lamps or abat-jours on sideboards, dressers or perimeter walls; direct with photocell inside the cabinet.

Furnishing

To furnish a modern bedroom it is also necessary to choose the right accessories.

In choosing the accessories I have some suggestions for you, also based on what I see proposed at trade fairs or by top-level companies and that I like. Here are some of them:

Absolute softness with a pouf matching the blankets.

Not everyone likes it, but I do: a rug is always a sophisticated idea of style.

The mirror furnishes; choose the right one that also widens the space.

A rocking chair: why not if the space is large?

Dressing table mon amour: there are some really beautiful vanities on the market for super chic bedrooms.

A fireplace for all tastes. The flame gives unprecedented warmth and atmosphere. If you don't have a chimney, an ethanol fireplace on a wall unit is also sufficient.

The curtains, I recommend, always in the same color and soft, very soft, possibly multi-ply.

Books, chairs, shelves with well-designed objects, never random things!

Paintings, small squares, photos: make them monochromatic so as not to interfere with the nuances of the room.

Now you have no more excuses not to make your bedroom truly extraordinary!

Turn your bedroom into a dream environment!

Painting the bedroom 5 pairs of colors that always work

- Paint the bedroom with just two colors

- Bedroom wall color matching

- The scale of browns combined with whites

- Woods with Stone Color

- White together with Black

- The Grays, but not too much

- Match a wallpaper

- Correctly match the colors in the bedroom

Some preliminary tips that I would like to give you before revealing the 5 pairs of colors that always work to paint a bedroom are the following:

If you want a "warm" bedroom, don't just think about the colors, but also and above all about the textures. Fabrics, textures, papers and decorations are elements that contribute to creating a rich, and therefore elegant, room.

Lacquered woods should be interspersed with veined woods or some texture to enrich the perception of the environment. In fact, all lacquered things could bring a "hospital room" effect.

All white looks good in magazines, but it's hard to manage.

All black ok, but only if you have a lot of light, so extra-large windows.

If you choose wallpaper, look for a relaxing pattern.

Avoid monochrome.

Also think about the blankets, sheets, duvets, pillows to coordinate. Paint the bedroom with just two colors

White bedroom

I'm often asked questions like:

What are the most relaxing colors for a bedroom?

The warmest, original, chic, calm colors for the master bedroom?

Or I'm asked for advice on the right painting for the classic or modern bedroom.

In short, everyone has their own mood!

A little secret: the bedroom has to be "vibrant" to look wow.

This means that the materials and their textures must be chosen with care.

Woods, metals, soft fabrics, and shapes that are not too rigid, help to create very interesting and unusual spaces.

Bedroom wall color matching

How to Match White and Beige Colors in the Bedroom

I like to think of a bedroom that remains beautiful over time, that is elegant and not tired after only 6 months.

Perhaps because it is a place of the heart, perhaps because superstitious people say that it is bad luck to change the wedding bed too often, but it is better to choose timeless furniture.

Whoever offers you orange, yellow or fuchsia in the relaxation room will also have their reasons, which I do not agree with.

The scale of browns combined with whites

These are very soft and timeless palettes, which evoke an elegant but not fashionable environment. It is no coincidence that it is a frequent combination in the chicest hotels, even 5 star ones.

Obviously, the whites (ivory, cream, optical white) are the prevailing colors, while the browns are used for fabrics, curtains, woods with important visible veins, accessories.

The choice of textures and materials must be careful and not too spartan.

It seems obvious to me that browns also include woods not tending to yellow or red.

In short, a look with an evergreen result that never has peaks of unmanageable or too bright tones, to confirm the elegance and refined look. You may also be interested in how to design interior paint combinations.

Woods with Stone Color

Wood has always been a top material, attractive and close to our most primitive visual and tactile needs.

Combined with stone, it creates a composition that ancestrally brings us back to environments with primordial energy, to the archetypes that we have handed down for generations. This pairing will never go out of style.

Combining the colors in the bedroom with these two materials is very simple: simple shapes, clean lines and a touch of softness with curtains and fabrics in linen and cotton.

If the stone is visible, all the better.

When the house is historic or has a rustic feeling, it is advisable to stop for a moment to reflect, so as not to distort the characteristics of the architecture that houses it.

My bedroom is in this style.

In reality, the bedrooms in historic houses deserve a separate note, in the sense that where the vaults are high or the architecture is very particular, or "present", one can dare with even darker or original tones.

Black & white is an ever-present combo.

The difficulty is to read it and apply it correctly.

There are many possibilities of interpretation, but the most effective is total black and white, without other interference colors.

As you can well imagine, however, it is a style that easily leads to errors: a complement or an out-of-tone fabric is enough to frustrate the whole layout.

The Grays, but not too much

Gray is also a color that is often used for elegant bedrooms.

Just think of Giorgio Armani's gréige (a mix of gray and beige, that is, a warm gray) which has become a symbol of refinement shared all over the world.

However, gray is a color that tends to cool and make the space plastic.

Use it only if you have a hardwood floor that gives warmth, or is mixed with a warmer, earthy color.

Create a combination that is beyond monochromatic, to prevent the room from feeling heavy right away.

Match a wallpaper

Wallpapers can also help complete the room.

Look for tone-on-tone designs so as not to weaken the nuances of the room.

If you want to be daring with color, make sure everything else is monochromatic.

I recommend not to overdo it with bright colors because a bedroom with too much chromatic energy disturbs the rest.

Correctly match the colors in the bedroom

I will reveal to you an effective method of verification to correctly match the colors in the bedroom. It is advisable to equip yourself with paper, pen, scissors and a little glue.

Let's say it's a hands-on approach to verifying that your ideas are indeed correct.

Get some newspapers or magazines.

Cut out pieces of floors, chairs, wardrobes, scraps of fabrics or colored pages according to the palette you want to give to your room.

Then stick them on a white sheet and let them settle for a few days.

If you still like them together, it means that you are on the right path. Otherwise, try other combinations.

You can also search for similar looks on Pinterest or Instagram.

Be careful to choose the right references because they often concern very large rooms or with details (doors, windows, lights) that are not exactly like yours.

When in doubt, first look for references, then create a composite with newspaper clippings.

Our rooms speak.

The bedroom is the most intimate room in the house, the one that "only we know" or only family members.

When the rooms begin to show the first signs of aging, it means that the work was not done as a work of art, in the sense that it is too close to the fashions of the moment or because a true style does not emerge. Find out how to combine colors for the bedroom.

How to Match the Colors in the Bedroom

The colors in the bedroom are important because they define the mood.

Today we can do without many elements, the rooms have shrunk a lot in size, so the colors must be defined well before buying wardrobes, beds, blankets and accessories and mixing them as best they can.

If you are lucky enough to design a house from scratch, you have a big advantage, being able to choose the one you like best and therefore you can create an original look & feel.

Otherwise, you will have to settle for what is there and act accordingly, more carefully.

Matching colors for bedrooms: how to choose according to age

Furnishing the room of children or teenagers seems a fairly simple task. In fact, they don't need complex furnishings, but how to choose the right color combination for the bedroom?

We know for sure that only a few boys and girls love the classic blue and pink.

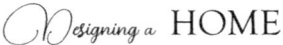

It is more a cultural heritage of ours, of the adults, that from birth we stereotype male children with blue, light blue and yellow and female girls with pink, peach and all the similar shades.

The first step you should take before decorating your son or daughter's bedroom, if he is in a more or less conscious age group, is to ask him / her what his / her favorite color is.

My children, up to 4-5 years old, categorically answered green. Growing up, the older one took different paths, preferring alternative colors, including even red.

That's right, it's not easy at all. On the one hand there are the tastes of the child, who watches Peppa Pig on TV and on Mondays loves pink piglets, or Paw Patrol, on Tuesdays he identifies with his favorite dog, choosing first yellow, then red and even the navy blue, in an infinite loop of colors.

On the other hand, there is the parent's search for simplicity and flexibility, who most often lived for 30 years in an orange or salmon bedroom, hating it to the bone, impatient to get rid of it.

Fortunately, today the choice is very wide and it is also quite tasteful, if you know where to buy from.

First of all we distinguish the various age groups of the child.

Small children (0-6 years)

Small children are easy to please. They care very little about colors at the end of the day. What they want in the room is an exorbitant mountain of games. They don't even care about the bed or the desk, to be honest.

For this reason, the advice is to choose a bedroom as like, without too many bows or decorations, you already know that they will end up being destroyed before the child learns to speak.

Use furniture made to measure for children and above all safe. Solid woods, Montessori bookcases and many, many rubber mats, called by us 'parquet-saving technicians.

You can begin to think about the wardrobe as something semi-definitive, that is, that the child will carry around until adulthood. But be careful here too not to fall into the multicolor trap. It counts that the child will have to put away their shirts, skirts and jackets even at 18 years old. I don't know if they would like to do it in a polka dot wardrobe or with the butterfly's screen printed onto it!

Make an effort to choose something at least minimalist.

To protect the walls, you can opt for a wallpaper that can also be removed or for chalkboard colors on which they can express their first Picasso instincts.

Children age 7-14

It is the age when ego begins to impose itself both in clothing and in private spaces. In this age group it is advisable to involve the boy or girl and satisfy their tastes, more than anything else to avoid retaliation and long faces.

 Choose together the shape of the bed, the arrangement of the desk and even the playful part, with computer and hobby space (I already know that technology will be a great component).

It is interesting to see how bedroom companies propose solutions that are close to the psychology of those who will experience it. There is the room of the explorer, that of the dancer, that of the scientist, of the aspiring fashion blogger.

We know that the teenager identifies a lot in the role of his hero or friend. Indulging these tastes is important.

However, it should be borne in mind that:

- the use of bright or impractical colors will make the bedroom "age" quickly

- the space must be made comfortable. If the bedroom is large, do not hesitate to use a larger bed

- bridge solutions are to be considered only in cases of extreme necessity

Boys age 15-20

Choosing the colors of the bedroom for a teenager is a seemingly easier task, only because the adult should abstract himself from the decisions and have the boy / girl create his own space.

In this case it is easy to understand that it is no longer a bedroom, but a real grown-up person's room. A bookcase, roomy wardrobes and a comfortable bed can be comfortable, but no longer for a child.

Personalization always depends on the aptitudes of the individual, whether he loves art, machines, the Playstation or reading. The advice is to enliven the walls with large format prints, perhaps themed.

Today on the market there are almost all colors available, so it seems easy to furnish the bedroom.

Personally, as you can see from my projects, I prefer pastel colors that are not too "flashy". Sage green, dusty blue, antique pink, woods and lots of white.

Depending on how you arrange the furniture, you can adjust the walls accordingly. I don't like excessive color, I find it too fashionable and difficult to manage. I prefer soft tones and paint on one / two walls.

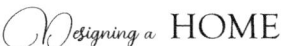

Wallpaper and color block

I often use a mix of wallpaper and color, find out how to combine them here. I like to cover only some parts with paper, to make them stand out. For example, 1-meter wide strips at full height, interspersed with bands of color.

In this way the room will seem original, not obvious.

I also frequently use the color block technique, which consists in painting only some parts with one color, such as rectangles or partial circles. This is a very simple technique that customers like in the bedroom.

Remember that clutter is the first way to make the bedroom look unplanned and chaotic. Avoid at all costs things left here and there, piles of toys scattered around and clothes stacked on the bed. Design closed containers that facilitate the order, so that everything has its place.

In terms of accessories, you can look for baby lights, cute coat hanger knobs, containers on wheels, baskets and chests.

Never impose limits on your imagination!

KITCHEN

Furnishing a classic contemporary kitchen: ideas and inspirations

---

The salient feature of the contemporary classic is that it is a mix of elements + classic decorations and very clean shapes + lines, together with modern materials.

How much classic is there and how much contemporary, is up to you.

In choosing a contemporary classic kitchen, 3 main factors influence:

- the lines, which must be a perfect mix of classic moldings and contemporary shapes;

- the materials, which take a lot from the classic (marbles, woods, metals, and bronze);

- the mood, which has a different flavor compared to both styles, classic and contemporary, taken individually.

In general, contemporary classic kitchens are smaller than they used to be, in which the kitchen area even exceeded 50 square meters.

Being more compact and technologically more advanced, it is normal that their structure is different from the purely classical style.

Strategically speaking, from a design point of view, the contemporary classic kitchen can be of two main types:

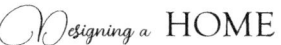

- Very contemporary, let's say minimalist, with only materials from the classical repertoire.

- Contemporary in the lines, but with some more classic decorations, in a measured way.

The first type is simple to understand.

No handles, simple doors, refined materials. Few pieces, almost all the same and shapes really reduced to the bone.

This strategy is mainly used when you want to emphasize different elements in the rest of the open space, for example a particular sofa or boiserie on large walls.

It is a sort of "stylistic balance": we prefer to reduce the classic dose in the kitchen to enhance it elsewhere.

It can be very effective in small houses, where having a lot of classic is really heavy.

The second type is more distinctive. The kitchen is no longer so simplified, moldings, decorations (albeit in small doses) and refined materials appear, and the scheme is enriched with personality.

When to choose a classic contemporary kitchen?

When you are simply fed up with being too modern and you want something "warmer" in form.

It is well known that contemporary kitchens are now ubiquitous in showrooms.

They can be found in all colors, you can find them at the house of friends, of the aunt who has renovated, of your former classmate. Some kitchens, especially the totally white ones, are everywhere.

A bit like plaster spotlights. They are now within everyone's reach.

If you want something more refined, less obvious and closer to your taste, as long as you like the concept, you have to opt for the contemporary classic.

Obviously, being an unconventional style, try to get the best advice and avoid DIY.

Any mistake could affect the final design of your kitchen.

Sometimes it happens that you already have a classic kitchen and want to "just modernize it a bit".

Well, you won't necessarily succeed.

It always depends on the type of classic of the original kitchen, that is, if it is just the doors or if it is full of decorations, columns, moldings, pilasters and various baroque styles. In this case it will be difficult!

If the materials in which it is made are disused woods, such as cherry or beech, you can have the doors lacquered and bring it back to life.

Try to replace or eliminate the handles, which are a stylistic impediment, or to make them very minimal, in chromed steel or gold.

I also recommend that you review the composition.

Today kitchens are quite compact, there is not much room for walking around. Eliminate everything that is not themed and replace it with something new, which resumes the desired style.

The molded doors could be only in the bases or only in the wall units. You can think of breaking the surface up with a stoneware or marble top like in this composition below.

If your kitchen has slightly worn doors, you can decide to keep them, paint them and replace tops and appliances.

You will probably have to change a few pieces, modernize something else, light it better and give it a new look. It is not impossible!

If, on the other hand, the hardware leaves something to be desired, the doors are made of unidentified material, or it is simply not worth contacting a carpenter for restyling, then change it first.

Kitchen shops, in fact, are reluctant to adapt: it is often a long and risky job, it is not worth wasting your time on old things!

Some companies offer models that can be adapted well if you want to furnish a classic contemporary kitchen.

In the choice of materials, you choose both lacquers (matt and glossy) and woods, but do not neglect the metal-effect lacquered aluminum, glass and marble.

In terms of colors, in addition to whites and blacks, there are also new and refined colors, such as cashmere, silk gray, mud, champagne, copper and other shades that are not already "too seen". In the kitchen there is not only white!

Matching the color of the kitchen with the floor: all the chicest combinations

- Matching the color of the kitchen with the floor: to be or not to be?

- Kitchen combinations with gray floors

- Kitchen combinations with light or medium parquet floors

- Kitchen combinations with dark parquet floors

- Combinations of kitchens with stone floors

- Kitchen combinations with decorated or rustic floors

When it comes to matching the color of the kitchen with the floor, most people struggle.

It is certainly not easy, the fear of making a mistake in matching the floor is always lurking and, as the purchase of a kitchen is a considerable expense, there is always the fear of a false step, that in the end the result is not what was hoped for.

In this chapter I will review 5 possible floor-kitchen combinations depending on the material you already have at home or are about to assemble, if you are close to a renovation or a new building.

I warn you that the combinations are almost infinite, as you can well imagine, but I will try to simplify some concepts to allow you to understand what you like and what works.

Matching the color of the kitchen with the floor: to be or not to be?

Hamletic doubts hover over the decisions to be made. Here you will find a practical guide for those who want to change the floor.

Is it better a dark or light kitchen? Better a wooden floor? ... A wooden kitchen or a white kitchen? And what if the two woods in the kitchen go badly together?

Here, questions and uncertainties are on the agenda.

Let's clarify, in order.

Kitchen combinations with gray floors

It sounds rare, but actually a lot of you have a gray floor at home. I feel like the famous "50 shades of gray" are more popular than ever!

In this case you basically have two ways out if your floor is stoneware, resin, stone or a gray marble.

You can (which I recommend) buy a kitchen with warm wooden references, or, alternatively, choose a totally neutral look.

In the first hypothesis, the kitchen will be "warmed" by the grain of the wood, possibly light or medium, which will interrupt the flattening given by the monochromatism of the floor.

In the second hypothesis the result will be minimalist, effective in contemporary environments where, for example, there is a beautiful view of a garden or large windows with a super panorama. Ideal for those who want a minimal, ultra-contemporary and a little cooler home. You may also be interested in how to furnish a classic contemporary kitchen.

The totally neutral look with gray flooring is often seen in American penthouses or lofts, those with a view of skyscrapers or in the middle of nature. In this case, the exterior helps a lot, so it makes no sense to climb into too complicated combinations of colors and materials.

Evaluate the choice on the basis of your tastes and the light available in YOUR apartment.

Here the discussion becomes more interesting!

The wooden or wood-effect floor is a material that already fills and warms by itself, making it apparently easier to match with the right kitchen.

The vast majority of you choose a white kitchen in order not to be mistaken. The result is still warm and it's very easy to decorate with neutrals!

Lately there are also alternative approaches that see the use of black kitchens. They are not as widespread, but black in the house is becoming more and more popular.

The real difficulties arise when you have to match a color or another wood to the parquet floor.

What color, what wood?

Here doubts arise.

When you have a wooden floor and you want to put wood into the kitchen you have to pay attention to these two steps:

Choose a wood of the same tone.

Detach the wood from the floor, perhaps inserting it in the wall units or in the top and not directly on the bases. Read also 'How to choose the right materials for the tops, doors and splash guards.

There is also a third thing you can do, which is to call an architect, but it seemed too obvious to me!

If, on the other hand, you want to give a touch of color to the kitchen with a wooden floor, you can choose a shade that is not too bright and that is in a palette with the colors you have chosen for the room.

In general, staying neutral is always a strategy that works, but a touch of color (teal, copper, sage green ...) is not necessarily indicated.

Kitchen combinations with dark parquet floors

The dark parquet manages to give a beautiful effect to the environment, but complicates things a bit in terms of combinations.

Generally, it is better to opt for furnishings with light colors. A dark kitchen would look great on an aesthetic level, but it could burden the space.

As you can see, the combinations that work best are the lighter ones.

Certainly, when you decide to furnish with a dark parquet you have to pay attention to the lighting. In fact, there must be good natural light

first of all and then also the artificial lighting must be well studied, perhaps by a professional.

Dark parquet woods work just as well. As I explained for the situation with light parquet, in general the woods should never be combined (bases + floor) and the same shade must be chosen. This does not mean that the wood must be identical, but that it must not turn yellow or red.

Matching kitchen floor color

Matching the kitchen color with the floor is a game of shades indeed!

If the floor is a beige or a stone effect, the combinations are very simple. Neutral tones are ok, as are whites, blacks and woods.

Let's say that such an effect on the floor (stone or warm resin, beige) is one of the easiest and most effective mixes that exists in the contemporary world, so combining the furnishings becomes truly versatile!

You can keep it light or add dark woods or colors. Everything works. Read also how to decorate with dark floors.

Kitchen combinations with decorated or rustic floors

I have already spoken here of furnishing combinations with difficult floors.

If the floor is particularly decorated or rustic, keep it simple. You can insert woods, colors and metallic or white effects, but the final effect will change depending on the actual decoration you have on the floor.

A kitchen with a very jagged or decorated floor (cement tiles, decorations with figures), is good to keep minimalist, both in colors and shapes, so as not to complicate the design too much.

If, on the other hand, the floor, even if decorated, has a simple overall effect, you can dare with some more textures and colors, to give that touch of personality that is missing.

Which combination do you like best?

All the combinations to furnish modern kitchens with style and taste

What are the combinations to furnish modern kitchens with style and taste?

The kitchen, as we know, is a constantly evolving home environment.

Just think about how they have transformed over the years. Our mothers had small kitchenettes in the 70s completely separated from the dining area, where they worked in tight spaces.

Gradually kitchens have opened up and have clearly improved in appearance and usability, up to the current open spaces, which combine kitchen and living room. A remarkable revolution, which has changed the way of living and conceiving the operational and functional environment.

The first islands were born, directly modeled on Anglo-Saxon kitchens, which gradually became a must-have of contemporary Italian cuisine.

What awaits us in the years to come? How do you choose the right color, combination, material according to your tastes and possibilities? Let's see some interesting news.

Three interesting novelties for the kitchen concern those who have large spaces and want to invest in design and extreme functionality. This is the introduction of the double island, one of which plays a more functional role, ideal for food preparation and can include a second sink or even an additional dishwasher.

Of course, the main attraction of having two islands is that you have double the operating space!

The second island is mostly dedicated to eating or entertainment. It often has a stool area, which allows guests to relax while you prepare a meal or your kids to do their homework while you prepare an after-school snack.

Another advantage of this design feature, which mostly affects high-end kitchens is that the double island can help you fill the space in large rooms (see villas), give you more storage container elements (eliminating pantries and closets) and even better manage household appliances such as wine racks or double refrigerators.

This type of kitchen looks perfect for a large family who spends a lot of time in the area.

The two islands can be parallel, adjacent or a T. The "top" of the T is generally the work island, while the "stem" acts as a table area. The two islands can be connected, or they can be separated by a few meters.

Monolithic island kitchen

Another alternative is a large, multifunctional island, with a monolithic appearance. Kitchen manufacturers are investing heavily in technological innovation for upholstery materials that have a continuous appearance. As if a 90x150cm block of marble or stone had "accidentally crashed" into your living area!

At the design level, such a kitchen is absolutely spectacular, even if such materials add to the costs a little.

Let's say that having a large space available is an added value that facilitates composition, but even in medium-sized kitchens it is possible to obtain extraordinary results.

Concealed kitchen

A strategy that concerns small kitchens is to make them retractable, or closable. The introduction of the roto-translating doors has made it possible to innovate the layout for all those who do not like an open kitchen or in cases where the kitchen is right in front of the entrance to the house.

Generally, those who choose such a layout prefer order and cleanliness to practicality, and often combine a walk-in pantry in which to arrange everything needed to make up for a minimal kitchen, also combined with a small laundry.

There are two most interesting trends in this sense for 2022.

The first concerns the use of earth tones or neutral materials instead of the usual white.

The inspiration comes from the shades of the natural environment such as cappuccino, dove gray, beige, rust, clay, terracotta and even green. Let's say that it is an evolution compared to the usual white, which is now almost omnipresent in the homes of Italians.

More and more customers are choosing kitchens with lacquered glass doors. The glass gives a refinement and an inimitable design elegance compared to other materials. The structures are lighter and the glass has a simpler handling.

The second concerns the use of dark and cold colors, such as black, graphite, anthracite or blue. This is mostly a design attitude that concerns large kitchens with a warm floor (eg parquet or marble).

Fewer and fewer families fear the impact that a dark kitchen can have at home, indeed, they prefer it to the Scandinavian white that we inherited from the 2000s. It is no coincidence that the major manufacturers of high-end kitchens always have a luxury line that enhances the dark tones.

White or contrasting marble (or marble effect) is the most used material for those who want to achieve a luxury look.

Gold, copper and black faucets are sure to make headlines in 2022. It's always about the personal taste, look and pattern you want to bring to your kitchen, but attention to detail allows you to take the leap.

Splashbacks are fast becoming a 5-star choice in kitchen design.

Trendy in 2022 is definitely a splash guard with a window overlooking your garden!

If you can't have it for architectural reasons, consider inserting a splash guard in continuity with the top. Very often stoneware is chosen because it is one of the most resistant and beautiful materials for the kitchen.

Best kitchen materials to choose tops, doors and backsplashes

Let's say that the continuity between the top and the splash guard is a very interesting must. In fact, the classic "tile" that breaks the continuity of the material is no longer used, but a more monolithic and designed look is preferred.

The backsplash in general should be a breaking point with respect to the floor, looking for a contrast so as not to risk a result that is too "brown", too "wood", too "marble". Variation allows you to create an interesting mix.

If you have a wooden floor, it makes no sense to overload with too much wood in the doors. Thin out the design and use doors and tops of other materials, with at most a few veins.

If you have a marble or stone floor you can look for a good combination of veins and colors. Don't overdo it with tones that are too beige, interrupt them with some cold tones.

THE BATHROOM

---

7 Chic Solutions to Decorate the Bathroom in 2021

If you're in the mood for renovations or need to build your bathrooms from scratch, you can consider these contemporary trends to create a fresh new look.

TRENDS IN 2021 ARE OF THREE BASIC TYPES:

More color: bathroom fixtures with bright colors, adding artwork or wallpaper in bold shades of green, yellow, pink, blue.

More mimimalism: do not cover all the walls, or use only light coatings, such as enamel paints or resins.

More elegance: use of marble (or marble effect) with a glossy touch, combined with parquet flooring and lots of white.

DECORATE THE BATHROOM

Whatever your style, whether you are looking for a trendy bathroom, a natural space or a decorated look, you can read this chapter to get a better idea.

GAME OF ELEGANT IMITATIONS

Marble effects (and real marbles, of course) are hugely trendy lately. If I can express an opinion, the final result is very elegant, provided however that you choose a large format slab, equal to or greater than 100x100cm, preferably extended vertically, eg. 100 × 300.

The problem of having a small-sized marble covering is the repetition of the pattern, which creates a rather boring "drawer" texture on the wall.

COVERING THE BATHROOM WITH LARGE CALACATTA GOLD SLAB

However, the marble-effect stoneware wall tiles remain one of the most popular because they bring back a material that has always been precious, eliminating the problems of managing real marble.

It is a very versatile material that is available in many variations, some of these very realistic, and which allows you to create a chic bathroom without a huge expense.

Marble is always well combined with gold or bronze accessories and taps.

GROOVED SURFACES

This is a trend that is still not very evident, but which will take shape in the coming months. These are ceramic or wood claddings that have vertical or horizontal strip grooves, similar to cuts or ribs, so as to create a vibrant chiaroscuro effect on the wall.

I have already talked about wooden strips to be used as dividers, but in the bathroom, it is mostly ceramic or wall decorations, or surface finishes of bathroom furniture.

The most obvious objection is the lack of practicality regarding dust: in reality they are non-absorbent ceramics, so if you place them in the shower with grooves placed vertically, they are as practical as any other covering material.

I like them a lot!

The visual decorative trend is perfectly palpable in 2021. On the one hand there are fiberglass wallpapers on the market, on the other hand there are also extra-large format stoneware that becomes more and more representative and similar to wallpaper, even though remaining ceramic materials.

This approach is perfect for those who don't want a boring bathroom, but always colorful or with a "wow" effect.

DECORATIVE EFFECT WITH LARGE-FORMAT STONEWARE SLABS

Here, too, chooses a large-format slab that allows you to avoid the infinite repetitiveness of a small pattern, which could be alienating in the long run.

Homeowners have become more and more courageous in their bathroom choices.

People want to be different and have bespoke touches, colorful ceramics or unique settings that create a detachment from the past.

EVERGREEN JUNGLE

A touch of green in the bathroom has always been liked by many, let's face it. Whether it's a "real" green, with real plants or flowers, or a jungle effect through wallpaper, the idea of having a bathroom inspired by Bali scenography gives a sense of tranquility and escape, especially these days.

The jungle is very popular with both the most romantic followers, with large printed flowers, and the youngest, who will find themselves totally projected into a sort of earthly paradise, even if they are alone in the shower.

A style tip: if you choose a very evident pattern, don't repeat it psychedelically on all the walls, but choose to cover only one part or simply the inside of the shower.

LESS IS MORE

Contrary to the trends we have seen, there is always the trend of minimalists, that is of those who want a bathroom that "lasts a hundred years", outside the fashions of the moment. It is an almost masculine approach, of those who prefer practicality to a design that is too obvious.

If you find yourself in this group, choose to cover the bathroom with a sober coating, for example a large resin-effect slab, or the actual resin. With these new systems you can say goodbye to too patterned decorations and leave room for a timeless, albeit "flatter", elegance.

COVER THE BATHROOM WITH RESIN AND WALLPAPER

A tip: if you decide to opt for resin, create some element of attraction in the furniture to ensure that the eye does not get lost when looking at a completely single-color bathroom. Play a lot with hidden lights to achieve a pro effect.

NEW CLASSICISM

A touch of classic can be obtained both with the marble effects that we have already seen, and with a "terrace" design, or even with repeated small-format tiles.

Classic accessories with beautiful shapes and soft and elegant colors

harmonize well especially when there is a contrast between a light (eg

the tub) and a dark one (eg the floor). For a sense of grandeur, introduce

at least one "wow" effect feature: a mosaic or a huge mirror is especially

nice in a Renaissance-inspired setting.

DECORATE THE BATHROOM

No longer relegated to just magazines, gold is back and catching on as you explore your glam side in the bathroom. An easy way to introduce gold in moderation is to introduce it gradually. Start with a faucet or lamp, then try more accessories if you haven't got enough yet.

Remember, you need to try to coordinate essential materials, rather than burdening the scene.

Wood is an excellent starting point for the bathroom, in a natural and material way. The natural and non-industrial finishes offer just the right respite from the hard and cold surfaces commonly found in the bathroom.

Select darker woods or concrete elements on a rough surface. The idea is that there is at least one material finish to recreate the tactile factor lost with surfaces that are too smooth or shiny.

While color is key to creating a personal space, fans of natural and monochromatic interiors need not fear thanks to an emerging trend coined Japandi, defined by a combination of minimal Japanese style and simple Scandinavian accents.

Minimal natural styles are perfect for an essential look, especially through wood, pebbles, stone and many tactile textures.

How to furnish a modern bathroom: 5 trends to copy

If you are looking for ideas to furnish a modern bathroom, know that bathroom furniture trends, as well as trends in the home and furniture environment, do not develop in a very short time.

In fact, they are mostly launched during the annual home design fairs and events and then gradually assimilated by magazines and by many companies in the sector, which adapt to market demands.

A bit like in the fashion world, but in a slightly more gradual way.

The past few years have seen a triumph of the Scandinavian house. Oak everywhere and a lot of white, as an icon of the new minimalism.

This type of house is transforming. "It's a bit boring", as some of my clients say.

The Scandinavian house today is enriching itself with details, it is no longer so minimalist and it is no longer so totally white.

On the one hand there is (and will continue to be) the Nordic style, which has a strong hold on Italians, especially those with small houses.

On the other hand, since last year, a more elegant and even quite dark type of house is becoming more and more popular.

The need for a well-organized and refined environment is also spreading in the bathroom sector, where materials and customizations take on priority.

Let's see in detail the 5 trends to copy if you need to renovate your bathroom.

Height development

Making the most of your space, especially for small bathrooms, is a must.

If the size of the bathroom doesn't allow you to fully express yourself, make it a well-organized space with personal touches and floor-to-ceiling furnishings.

In fact, these last few years have seen the triumph of custom-made wardrobes, partially open, which allow you to store everything, from linen to brooms, without losing even an inch.

Empty bathrooms are a possible feature in large homes. The minimal ones, on the other hand, take full advantage of all the angles. There are those who get rid of the bidet (through the use of a hand shower) to make room for an extra container.

Accent walls

The bathroom is also to be considered like a bedroom. The accent walls, i.e. those to be made protagonists to enhance the space and concentrate the visual point towards a main element, can be studied according to the shape of the room and the priority that you want to give to the elements.

Generally, the wall of the sink, tub or shower is highlighted, leaving that of the sanitary ware in the background.

Even in the bathroom it is possible to correct any defects by painting a wall darker, as explained in this post.

In the bathroom the accent wall can be made with a different material or color to contrast the others. The most frequent choices are marble, stoneware of another color, mosaic, natural stone and even wallpaper, in many cases.

You can paint your wall black, for example, and it will work the same way. For a more modern look, you can use backlit mirrors as an accent wall - you have no limits of choice!

Diffused lights for a modern look

Light is the element that makes the bathroom very interesting. With continuous advances in lighting technology, we are now able to integrate lighting into architecture in ever more exciting and effective ways.

Enough with the usual light bulbs in the center of the room or ceiling lights without quality! The light in the bathroom must be studied, conceived and designed.

A practical example could be to illuminate the beauty area with a diffused light behind the mirror, a direct suspension next to the sink and a false ceiling to insert spotlights and luminous cuts.

In short, these bathroom furniture trends see a multiplication of light sources in order to make the space more articulated and interesting.

New textures

In terms of coatings, there is now a bit of everything on the market. Very small formats, colors and textures of all types and all facets, marble, wood, resin, colored, glossy, opaque, lapped, gold effects and so on and so forth.

Among the countless proposals, there is the return of travertine, a marble that has been snubbed in recent times and is always very elegant, and the tendency to mix materials and types of coverings, even contrasting ones.

For example, a resin wall, one covered in stoneware, another just painted. There are no limits to the imagination.

The opposites work as a coating method: coat all or only half coat or no coat at all. The coverings up to 210cm are losing a bit, because with full-height furnishings they are rather uncomfortable and unsightly.

At the level of color, there is no particular trend that prevails. However, we can divide the design choices into two strands: the simple and sober ones and the more dramatic ones (which I'll describe later).

The simple trend involves the use of pastel colors, earth colors or neutral and light veins.

Even the furnishings are enriched with new textures capable of furnishing without adding much else.

Metal always has the function of enriching an environment. Snubbed until a few years ago, today it is back in vogue especially in its color variations. Edged mirrors, gilded taps, bronze suspensions and accessories... many effects that make the environment super chic.

Especially if you choose wood-colored or lacquered bathroom furniture, the metal serves to greatly enrich the palette and to increase the reflections that make the environment chicer.

If you want to change your look without throwing away the tiles, I recommend that you take a closer look at your bathroom and

1. if it has not very contrasting colors

2. if it has lacquered or veined furniture and

3. if it is not very bright, you can decide to add a metal mirror, a few vases or original reflective accessories, or you can change the taps.

The dramatic look.

For those who want to dare, the "dramatic" look is an original touch to try in very small bathrooms. If you are planning a bathroom and want

something new you can opt for a strong look with the addition of interesting tiles, in a dark tint or through the use of wallpaper to create a wow effect, and unexpected mood.

The dramatic look itself is dark. The floor alone or the internal shower lining alone can help create a super original look & feel, to be imitated.

Minimal taps and sanitary ware

While on the one hand the coverings and wall treatments will be the protagonists of 2021, on the other hand the sanitary ware and taps will be increasingly minimal, intent on blending in with the rest of the bathroom.

Faucets identical to the shower box, colors to match the sanitary fixtures: the range of finishes has been greatly expanded.

The forms, on the other hand, are highly simplified.

Attention is focused on increasingly functional and technologically advanced accessories. The bathroom in the 2021 furniture trends finally takes on a leading role, never of service. As such it requires an unprecedented dignity and look, whatever size it is.

MODERN CURTAINS FOR INTERIORS: HOW TO CHOOSE THEM FOR EACH ROOM

Did you know that modern interior curtain designs can also help solve some décor issues?

Yes, even if the curtains seem to be the last of the accessories in order of purchase, in reality they must be designed in time, to help you create the perfect look.

What kind of curtains to hang?

In the ranking, if I had to choose the absolute best curtains in terms of style and look, I would prefer the soft curled curtains (not too much) in natural fabrics, with very light natural textures in sight. I would discard colors like yellow, red, damask and other oversized draperies a priori and focus on neutrals.

In some cases it is possible to use shades of green and blue, desaturated and, therefore, not lit. These are colors that fill the room a lot, so they should be used sparingly (and always coordinated with the rest of the furniture).

For the living room I would definitely choose a soft curtain.

For the kitchen, a soft curtain or a roller blind, depending on your needs. The best approach is not to use too many types in the house, maximum 2, especially in adjacent rooms such as the kitchen and open space living room.

For the bedroom or children's room, a soft double-cloth curtain is better with the possibility of darkening the room easily.

Types of modern curtains

Let's go in order: what are the most common types of contemporary curtains?

Here they are:

- Soft or gathered curtains

- Roller blinds

- Roman blinds

- Panel curtains

- Venetian blinds (horizontal and vertical)

Soft curtains

They are certainly the most widespread and the most versatile, especially in the presence of French windows with frequent passage.

The drop curtains, or sheets, are used for elegant day and night rooms, with the possibility of making them fall sinuously onto the floor (about 10-15cm more). Not everyone likes this feature, for many it is not very hygienic, but it certainly makes the environment more refined and goes very well in large rooms with large windows.

The possibilities of design are many, from the single sheet to the double or triple one, with fabrics of all types and sticks of all shapes and materials.

For the overflowing floor models (not free-standing, soft) it is good to avoid the use of fabrics such as linen or cotton with asymmetrical or too wrinkled shapes because at the first wash they could lose their initial dimensions and be defective. As we know, linen tends to shorten and therefore the curtain itself could be compromised.

At the composition level, it is possible to accommodate one or more curls also to solve the problems of exaggerated brightness or privacy.

I like to use at least two / three sheets: a semi-transparent central one and one / two darkening lateral drops to complete the result.

If you choose a neutral color (white, gray, ivory, beige, dove gray ...) you do not need to recall the specific color in the furnishings or accessories.

Personally, I have a strong preference for calm and evergreen colors.

I like the passepartout colors and the types of very soft curtains, which by themselves create a seductive appearance in the environments in which they are placed.

If you choose to use completely white curtains, you can decide on a fabric with backlit textures, always preferable natural, such as those of fine linens and cottons. Damask, very evident floral or geometric designs are not a sign of great elegance.

Roller blinds

Roller blinds are blinds-not-blinds, used for large windows and able to darken without drapery, therefore easier to clean.

They are ideal for masculine, minimalist environments, with simple colors, or rooms where a lot of hygiene is needed, such as bathrooms and kitchens. The new mechanisms allow remote control, to avoid hassle.

Roller blinds for large windows

There are also twin roller blinds that alternate a covering band with a transparent one. They are practical for those areas that need light, but also need privacy.

Some models of roller blinds can be mounted directly on glass, in order to facilitate the opening of the door. This is an extreme solution, but not very chic.

Roller blinds solve space problems, because they are very compact, plus they tend to broaden the perception of the rooms, making everything much larger, but squatter.

Roman blinds

Roman blinds are a variant of the middle ground between canvas and roller blinds.

They are suitable for contemporary environments where you do not want to dare very much, but look for a softer solution than the roller.

Panel curtains

Panel curtains are an alternative to the soft curled curtain concept.

They consist of rigid sliding panels (wall or ceiling) suitable for large windows or situations in which it is necessary to vary the configuration of the shading during the day.

The panels can be customized and no string is needed to move them.

Venetian blinds

Venetian blinds can be horizontal or vertical and remain a timeless solution.

They are mainly suitable for office environments and create interesting light / shadow effects. The venetian blind is fixed to the wall or ceiling, covering the entire niche: a particularly decorative solution.

They can be remote-controlled or manual and when the slats are horizontal or perpendicular (in the case of vertical Venetian blinds) they allow a total view of what is happening outside.

Types of curling curtains

The curls can be different: kissed fold, flat fold, fan fold, or knotted, inclined and many other variations.

How to choose curtain color combinations

When choosing the colors it is good not to go too far from the palette of the room: for example, installing a red curtain in a total white interior is a gamble. The curtains must calmly accompany the colors of the interiors, differentiating themselves in tones and nuances, but never distorting the original chromatic composition.

Even highly decorated contemporary curtains with jungle or floral prints are no exception. The secret to coordinating them with the context is to use a color palette that characterizes the entire room. It is not good to choose a printed curtain without any of its tones present in the room.

The contemporary rods

In the modern home, the rods tend to be more and more concealed, or at least minimal.

In general, cuts are made in the false ceiling able to accommodate the rods, which in this way are very practical to hide.

In case of lack of false ceiling, you can use a linear and simple valance, a veil or frame, or a rod with a clean design.

The old wooden or iron rod with rings has been innovated by transforming itself into a metal tube of the most varied finishes and diameters. The new curtain systems have a steel wheel that rolls on a tube or cable whose diameter varies between 2 and 20 millimeters.

These curtain systems can be extended infinitely even in curved situations, thanks to the 'passing' shape of the support attached to the 'rolling' wheel.

The poles can be anchored both to the ceiling and to the wall, and today they also have the practical sliding system without the cord.

Just drag the curtain to create any style setup.

A curtain is necessary to hide radiators under the window, any not exactly aesthetic fixtures, irregularities in the openings (such as a higher door and a half-height door), roller shutter boxes and so on.

Generally, I recommend having the curtains made by a trusted upholsterer, who is available to take the measurements and to sew the fabric with precision and to the right size (the gatherings need more fabric).

It is not easy to order online, without seeing and touching the fabrics, seeing its transparency and color.

HOW TO COMBINE PARQUET: FURNISHING TIPS WITH FURNITURE, DOORS AND COLORS

How to match the doors to the floor?

Matching parquet with the rest of the furniture is just the beginning of interior design.

The complete process sees the style, the spaces, the color palettes of the house and much more as the protagonists.

In fact, combining parquet with furniture and other coverings is often complex and treacherous, it is no coincidence that it is one of the most frequently asked questions that I am asked along with which wooden floor to choose.

At least 80% of the questions I am asked concern the combinations between wood and other materials or colors.

I understand that, especially in DIY, doubts increase a hundredfold.

If you are "making your home", you will be called upon to quickly decide on your finishes and materials.

The company, for its part, will press to be able to proceed, you would like to take your time, but most of the time you have no way of immediately thinking about furniture. "I'll see to it later" - you find yourself exclaiming.

This attitude is understandable, but risky.

The finishes and colors, in my opinion, meld with everything else in the space.

You can't think in watertight compartments.

The risk is to lose personality or not to consider some fundamental elements that will make everything perfect.

But let's go in order.

How to combine parquet with furniture

The general rules to follow to match parquet with furniture, doors and all colors that look good.

First you need to consider your decor style.

You may also be interested in changing the floor to improve the style of your home.

- If your home is classic or chic, you can opt for dark colors.

- If your style is Nordic or minimalist, go for light colors, perhaps bleached.

- If your taste is industrial, you can choose a more lived-in wood.

In general, it is good to avoid too strong contrasts, especially between flooring and doors.

However, this does not apply to neutral colors, i.e. black and white, which go well with all floor colors.

An important piece of advice I would like to give you is that you absolutely must avoid risky combinations between parquet in the same

house, or the combination of real parquet and parquet-effect, and stoneware.

For example, it is not nice to see real wood throughout the house, then in the kitchen a detachment with a wood-effect, just for practicality.

As a way of thinking, light-colored parquet is more suitable for small houses.

Dark parquet floors, even with larger planks, look good in larger and brighter homes, because they have the characteristic of making the space seem smaller.

In my experience as an architect and interior designer, I happened to see dark parquet floors in very elegant and chic houses.

Nowadays there is no color or type of parquet that is more fashionable than others, precisely because of the different connotations of style.

Probably the most interesting parquet are those with very visible and tactile veins, almost to recreate a rustic effect.

Matching parquet with furniture, the secrets

I often say that choosing parquet should be more for men than for women.

Yes, because men are less emotionally involved, they are less paranoid about the perfection of an interior (except in exceptional cases!).

But then it is also true that women have a little more taste and pragmatism in choosing their home.

However, combining parquet with furniture does not have to be a stressful occasion.

Indeed, it must be a way to organize ideas, to understand the definitive style to give to your home.

SECRET # 1: FIRST OF ALL, EVALUATE THE "PRESENCE" OF YOUR PARQUET.

If you have an important wood, such as mahogany, wenge, or walnut or with an evident, marked grain, avoid combining it with materials and furnishings with as many rich woods.

In this way the eye will be attracted to a predominant element, the floor.

Also in this case, if you need to add a boiserie or a wardrobe, or design the doors, that is a vertical element with a large surface, do it by combining the essences as much as possible.

For example, do not use mahogany on the floor and yellow oak for the boiserie.

Use the same wood or a shaded wood, with a character more similar to a homogeneous surface (for example, an open pore lacquer).

SECRET # 2: DARK IS FINE, BUT DON'T OVERDO IT.

Unless you want a museum or vintage interior, don't go overboard with dark pairings. Dark wood tends to darken and darken, so it's not worth overdoing it in combinations.

A combination that is very strong, both in Scandinavian environments and in our areas, is dark wood on the floor with white on the walls and furnishings.

Especially when the wood is real and not wood-effect, the result is highly effective.

Match the parquet with the colors of the walls.

Here is another big question for who is going to furnish or renovate the house.

Here I'll tell you some of the most effective combinations to use.

Bleached wooden floor and light walls. The house will seem super spacious, even if you have to pay attention to the accessories to match so as not to make it feel cold.

Light Nordic wood flooring and dark walls. Ideal for very bright environments or with large windows.

Dark wood floor and light walls. Extremely elegant as a combination, the dark wood on the floor and walls + very light furnishings. Of great refinement, for minimalist homes, but difficult to build independently, for the desire to combine several materials together.

Dark wooden floor and colored walls. The color must be well dosed to avoid the pizzeria effect.

Dark floor, dark ceiling and light walls. It is not for everyone, but if well studied it can be very elegant.

Combining several woods, the right combination

Combining several woods, as I have already said, is not a problem.

It is enough to browse the most common furniture magazines to realize that some woods, even if not perfectly identical, still go well together.

SECRET # 3: IN ORDER NOT TO MAKE MISTAKES, COMBINE WOODS OF THE SAME SHADES.

Although not perfectly identical, the woods are quite versatile and only a very careful eye will observe the shading of two different woods.

The trick to avoid being kitsch is never to mix or put two too different woods too close together, for example one tending to yellow (oak) and one tending to red (mahogany).

These combinations may seem risky and inconsistent.

Make sure that the main furniture is the same shade.

For example, sofas, armchairs and coffee tables could all be built with a medium-toned wood, while lighter or darker colors can be featured with small accessories such as frames and lamps.

SECRET # 4: TRY TO DISTRIBUTE THE PIECES WELL SO AS NOT TO HAVE VERY STRONG WOODS CENTERED TOGETHER.

An environment must be as consistent as possible.

When you necessarily have to combine two different woods, make sure that they are well distributed inside the room.

Do not place them too prominently so that they are less noticeable.

How to match the doors to the floor?

While this topic deserves a separate post, there are two simple general rules for choosing doors correctly.

RULE # 1   CONTEMPORARY HOME

In the event that the floor of your home is dark in color and the context is contemporary, I recommend a door with very light or white colors, glossy lacquered. Better still if the door is borderless, linear or flush with the wall to blend in.

RULE # 2   CLASSIC HOUSE

In the case in which the parquet is rustic, vintage or classic, dark for example, the doors must have the same style, perhaps always in wood.

You can think of a decoration or boss on the door, even if the design remains minimalist.

As you will have understood, all these suggestions of mine are of a general nature.

It seems only right to tell you that drawing up a project is the only way to confirm or, even better, refute this attitude and create an interior with a wow effect!

Furnishing with turtledove: combinations and ideas to do it better

The dove-gray color is one of the most used and popular colors of recent years and furnishing with dove-gray has become the chromatic alternative for contemporary homes.

The neutral colors par excellence are known, they are white, black, gray, beige and for about ten years a particularly chic color has appeared in the palettes of interior designers, mixed between brown and gray, which allows a neutral result, but also warm and enveloping: dove gray.

This color has, like the more well-known intermediate shades, the characteristic of being a color able to match most of the furnishing styles and at the same time to create a refined and ageless environment.

In fact it is not invasive and dark, like brown, nor too light like beige, it does not tend to yellow or red, but it is a base to easily combine woods, lacquers and other materials.

This is why the dove-gray color was elected "the most loved color" for the interior walls of the house, immediately after white.

There is not only one turtle dove. The dove gray palette is diffuse and iridescent, depending on the brightness and the brown gradient that composes it.

The whole palette is in fact intriguing and is well suited to all types of rooms.

For small ones it is good to stay in rather light shades, because a dark dove can actually be heavy.

Dove gray, also called "greige" or "taupe", can be mixed in an infinite number of combinations with other more or less neutral colors, in order to create a very relaxing and elegant environment.

It can be used for furnishings, coverings or accessories and above all the latter manage to break the coldness caused by an environment that is too gray or totally white. See how to match the furnishings in a gray kitchen.

Taupe-colored curtains, cushions, and rugs are a very successful combination even in more modern rooms or in the presence of woods of another color. It is in effect a neutral shade: it goes well with any color.

FURNISHING WITH TURTLEDOVE: WHEN IT IS NOT CONVENIENT.

The turtledove has one drawback – it is flattening. Containing a high percentage of gray, the risk is to make the environment uninteresting if it were the only color present.

Another drawback is perhaps the diffusion of this color. Almost every home now contains dove gray furniture or wall.

Therefore, if you want to opt for a more original and unique effect, the combination with other materials must be well studied. Read also guide to designing paint combinations.

The best colors to combine with dove gray

Taupe and white

It is a chic and elegant combination that is bound to last a very long time. Especially in houses where there is parquet, it is a really interesting solution. Ivory is also worth evaluating. Less happy is the combination of dove gray and beige, destined more for classic or shabby environments.

Taupe and black

I am often asked how to break the "coldness" of an environment that has very dark or desaturated tones such as grays or blacks. The turtledove is a good solution. Even just for the accessories.

Taupe and gray

It is frequently found in sophisticated and luxury environments, such as hotel rooms or prestigious residences. It is not easy to manage, but, if well thought out, it guarantees a truly elegant effect.

Dove gray and whale blue

Having talked about how to decorate with blue, decorating with dove gray and whale blue, is rarer to find, but it is an interesting approach to

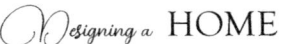

give the room a different, less obvious cut. You need to know how to dose the two colors well to create the right balance.

The turtledove has the advantage of being good with all kinds of colors.

I do not recommend combining it with the bright shades of yellow and red, while an alternative could be combining it with dark green for a very jungle-like and natural atmosphere.

This color is liked for the simple reason that it is very easy to find it in nature, which is why it is pleasant and never predictable.

To create a more interesting and chic effect, the ideal is to combine this color with the textures of wood.

In fact, especially in monochromatic environments, if the furniture were all lacquered or if the choice fell on completely opaque surfaces, the risk would be to generate an environment that is a little too cheap, therefore less interesting.

Dove gray should therefore be well balanced with woods, fabrics and textures that create a richer and more sophisticated look.

Another secret to creating a unique interior is to combine it with some shiny surface.

This means that the combination of dove-gray + glass (as a suspension can be) and dove-gray + marble is also perfect, for the contemporary classic style or for a table top, for example.

Being a color that is good in every style, it is necessary to set a palette of colors for each environment from the beginning and perhaps vary one color per room, keeping the rest of the palette constant.

It can be the right strategy to keep the whole house in warm and welcoming tones and give each room a different character.

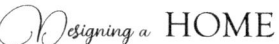

The sunroom & outdoor spaces

Sliding patio doors for exteriors: yes, or no?

Sliding patio doors for exteriors are a hotly debated topic. Can they be installed safely? Are they subject to authorization? What are the pros and cons of these systems?

Let's explore the issue of sliding or paneled windows, in which many of you, to tell the truth, are interested in all seasons.

Indeed, having already installed several, they are very practical. Basically, they serve to protect a terrace or balcony from wind and atmospheric agents and allow you to take advantage of an outdoor environment with more versatility and in any weather conditions.

SLIDING WINDOWS FOR OUTDOORS

One of the main advantages is that it is a system of mobile glass panels, without ground guide, with sash profiles without holes in the glass. So, you will understand very well that they are not invasive and do not require a hole in the floor.

You have the option of using single glazing up to 1.5 meters wide and the locking system is generally reliable. The windows in extra clear tempered glass allow you to close in a space without giving up the sunlight and avoid that "poor plastic veranda" effect.

This is an extra added value for any home or business.

A negative note: windows cannot always be installed easily.

Closing existing balconies, terraces, porches or loggias with windows is an intervention that certainly changes the appearance and functionality of a space.

THE CASE OF BIOCLIMATIC GREENHOUSES

The bioclimatic greenhouse is instead a space delimited by steel or iron windows and glass walls. It is an additional unheated space that allows the accumulation of heat coming from the sun's rays to be exploited as a support for the existing heating.

The veranda, which we talked about above, is a space obtained by partially or completely closing with glazed windows.

Both consist of glass walls adjacent to a building, but the bioclimatic greenhouse is aimed at saving energy which occurs through the accumulation of the sun's heat; the veranda, on the other hand, can be placed and oriented anywhere, it can have any cover and affect the volume of the house.

Furnishing the balcony: more than 70 ideas for an amazing look

The balcony can be considered as an expansion of your interior space and, secondly, it has an accessory function of relaxation, fun and, in general, more comfort.

Furnishing the balcony: the initial steps

Before you carry out any purchase, you should consider a few steps.

Paradoxically, low-cost furnishings could end up costing you more.

Buying balcony furniture at the lowest price doesn't have to be an automatic process.

You can certainly object by saying that garden furniture costs a lot, it's true, but most of the time it's because they have to be aesthetically beautiful, and above all in super weather-resistant materials and finishes.

Buying outdoor furniture involves more or less the same steps as buying pieces for the interior, but before starting to furnish the balcony it is good to make some additional considerations.

Furniture that is too cheap is often light, tends to yellow, is uncomfortable or not very durable.

Evaluate the weather and climate.

Is the climate hot and dry or do you live near the sea? Does it often rain?

All of these are important questions to answer before selecting furniture for the balcony.

Hot, dry conditions can cause wood to chip and crack.

So take into account that you will have to maintain it.

Even teak, a tough hardwood "for all seasons", will need to be treated annually to protect it from cracks and deformations. Strong winds can make aluminum accessories fly, and wicker will not withstand constant exposure to humidity: they are intended for covered outdoor spaces.

Moisture can also cause some metals to corrode.

Resin furniture, for example, is impermeable to different humidity situations and is available in many colors and finishes.

If there is too much sun, depending on the exposure, consider purchasing umbrellas, pergolas or sails to create some shade.

Furnish the closed balcony with windows.

Measure your space well.

Consider how much space you have and how it is shaped.

Do you have a long and narrow balcony or a large and wide terrace?

Study the shape of your exterior, terrace, patio or porch to determine the size of tables and chairs.

Make sure you leave enough space around for you to walk comfortably and apply the same principles for the flow of steps that you would use for interior décor.

In a narrow and long balcony a 80-90cm diameter bar table can work better than a normal dining set, because bar tables are narrower and stools take up less space than chairs.

Attention to comfort

When you are preparing to furnish the balcony, ask yourself first of all: what will be the function of my balcony?

Will it be a space to have lunch or to relax?

When seating, make sure you use a good quality, guaranteed, washable outdoor fabric that is resistant to fading, wind and mildew. Your cushions will stay at their best if you store them away when you no longer use them or in the colder months.

The accessories play a fundamental role in defining the final look.

An interior without accessories, vases, plants and floor lights always remains a bit bare.

Space to store furniture

Before thinking about how to decorate the balcony, make sure you can store your garden furniture somewhere for the winter.

Sometimes even partial covers won't provide you with enough protection, especially for materials like wicker.

Another option is to buy patio furniture that folds up and then cover it up for storage.

Evaluate the right lighting

Balconies often have an uninspiring appearance just because they are dark or poorly lit.

To furnish the balcony today the classic ceiling light in the center of the ceiling or applique on the wall is no longer enough.

Do not exceed 40-60 lux for the lighting of the plants on the balcony, in order not to risk glare.

You can use light garlands or floor lamps if you want to upgrade without having to buy a lot of accessories.

In general, I like to recreate a certain three-dimensionality of light to transfer the hierarchy of spaces into practical terms: if everything were strongly illuminated there would be nothing interesting, don't you think?

Change the floor

When furnishing a balcony, there are not only the furnishings, in fact even the floors are an important part of an exterior.

If the floor doesn't represent you at all or you don't like it anymore, consider laying a new one or making a floating deck with wooden planks.

Consider that the color of the floor is important to make a wow exterior. If you have a matchless floor, don't buy furniture in dubious colors, but focus on the final result.

Temporarily you can also use some nice outdoor rugs. Did you know that they exist and are widely used? Do not underestimate their decorative and aesthetic function.

Hide the ugliness

Air conditioners, deposits, boiler rooms: a big NO if they are visible!

When thinking about how to furnish the balcony, try solutions made on purpose or purchased to avoid perceiving the balcony as a second-hand warehouse.

If everything is in order and easy to clean, the eye sends feel-good impulses to the brain.

If there are too many colors and too many objects deposited without any function the effect changes a lot (for the worse).

Designing outdoor lighting: 30 modern ideas to illuminate the garden

Whether you are designing a garden from scratch, large or small, creating the perfect patio or simply looking for ideas, remember that effective and designer lighting is a must if you want to experience your outdoor spaces at night, during the long mild summer evenings or enjoy the outdoors even when the weather is cooler.

Three secrets for a rocking look!

First of all, I want to reveal to you three secrets to optimize the look of your outdoor space.

1. Focus your attention on plants and large furniture (seats, vases, tables...) and totally ignore what is unpleasant to the eye (eg a shed in the background, an unfinished railing...). The touch of class is always not to overdo it: it illuminates only the best pieces, because even a small light makes a lot of difference in the dark.

2. Divide the garden into areas. For example, identify the access routes, the main routes, the most reserved areas and the most decorative ones. Each area will need different lighting and different treatments for the best result.

3. If you are completely disoriented, experiment with a flashlight. To understand which areas of your garden, need to be better illuminated, take a torch in the evening / night and illuminate the various areas, pots, plants, seats, architectural forms. You will be able to check the different angles and understand which is the best for each scenographic element.

To start, you will need to think about lighting the trees, especially those with interesting bark, such as an olive or a birch. To create maximum impact, place a 50-watt spotlight near the base of the trunk so that the beam creates a play of light / shadow through the branches of the tree.

This type of light from the bottom up is particularly dramatic, but very effective because it immediately gives the feeling that the general lighting has been designed and taken care of, without improvisations.

In case you want to create dreamlike, fairy lighting, you can think of making suspensions or garlands of light rain from the branches of the most voluminous trees, placing a seat or a table immediately below.

During a party it can be a lot of fun and particularly suitable for photographs. Choose warm lights to create a soft and welcoming atmosphere.

By lighting it, you will let your garden become an extension of the interior even when it is night. Therefore, use light in a decorative way to highlight different shapes and particular characteristics.

To achieve a striking look, not only light is needed, but also shadows. So, dose the highlights sparingly.

Eventually you can add a warm and welcoming touch with hanging lanterns. Use colorful twine, thread or ribbons to hang them in the right place, or if you want a chic setting, mark the paths with minimalist floor-standing lanterns. You can find several at Maisons du Monde or on Amazon.

Another fundamental point is to illuminate the paths.

If you have built paths, such as walkways in wooden platforms, you can have holes made for small path marker lights.

Path lighting has two functions: a stenographic one, and a safety one. Thinking of lighting the trees and keeping the rest in the dark is a gamble. The path in the garden must always be highlighted, even if with weak lights.

Remember that all the lights you put in contribute to the atmosphere. Then proceed by priority, first lighting the functional parts (paths, entrances, patios, swimming pools) and then the suggestive ones (trees, walls, borders).

The paths can be illuminated with recessed spotlights (floor or wall) or with lamps that are fixed to the ground and can also be adjusted or camouflaged in the garden.

The entrances and therefore the doors, gates, intercoms, driveways and the like must be illuminated with wall lights and / or floor lamps at a height that is not too low to signal the walkway.

Garden lights work directly connected to the mains or via a transformer that supplies a low voltage current. There are also solar powered lights that can illuminate the most remote parts of the garden and can also be moved according to the seasons or needs.

Wireless solar powered LED lights have created a revolution in garden lighting, as they are increasingly commercially available, even in extremely different styles, economical and with low maintenance requirements. Solar lights offer up to six hours (and more) of lighting.

Light up the tables

As you already know, outdoor dining tables also need direct light, therefore a suspension or a point that illuminates the table from above.

Depending on how it is positioned, you can use suspended lights attached to a pergola, floor lamps or fun lights.

Illuminate the seating

The seats can be illuminated in different ways: with wall lamps, floor lamps, table lamps and / or even with luminous furnishings, such as vases or the seats themselves. Some examples are the furnishings of Serralunga, in polyethylene, which light up inside and make the environment particularly inviting.

Light up the barbecue

If for you summer means having friends in the garden for grilling and barbecues, you will need to light up your cooking area. Think functional lighting in this case - a well-placed spot that doesn't cast a shadow on the grill will be the solution.

Another idea could be to combine the seats with an outdoor brazier. There are many on the market, they can make up for poor outdoor lighting in the garden and create an atmosphere by warming the colder evenings.

The IP Protection Degree

When you buy an outdoor lighting fixture you must take into account the IP protection degree, which if not suitable for the application, can lead to problems, even serious ones, for the safety of the lighting system.

In fact, IP expresses the ability of a lighting fixture to resist atmospheric agents, both solid and liquid.

It is generally indicated with the initials IP followed by two numbers (eg. IP65), of which the first digit indicates the protection against the risk of penetration of solid bodies (dust, mold ...) and therefore also against the possibility of accidental contacts from a user, while the second digit indicates protection against the penetration of liquid substances (rain, water...).

In general, for normal outdoor installations there are products on the market with a degree of protection ranging from IP44 to IP68: for example, the lighting body with IP44 has a less valid protection against the penetration of water than an IP45 or an IP46, but can be used safely if not exposed directly to rain.

Get inspired!

MODERN OUTDOOR GAZEBO: THE CHICEST IDEAS FOR THE GARDEN

Modern outdoor gazebos, pergolas and the lighter shade systems with curtains and sails are an excellent pretext to arrange the outdoor area and experience a truly elegant summer.

Spring is the right time to start revolutionizing the terrace or garden!

Let's see them all in detail to get to know them better and get to the heart of the topic.

The pergola

Generally light, in wood or metal, it is an open structure both on the sides and in the upper part, without foundations, of modest size and easy to remove, whose purpose is to create shade by means of climbing plants, straws or sheets.

Tent

Regardless of the size, it serves to improve the daily usability of an existing space, such as a balcony or part of a garden. Its installation is always free of building interventions.

The gazebo

It is a covered architectural structure, open on the sides, usually fixed and built-in structural wood, wrought iron, or masonry. If intended to

meet permanent needs, a building permit is required. Otherwise, it is a free building for which landscape authorization is not usually required.

The pergotenda

Similar to a curtain, it is an external furnishing structure, consisting of a light and removable metal or wooden structure with a small section, covered by a retractable cloth, cane or bamboo mats or transparent film material, free of masonry and closed walls of any kind, consisting of light elements, assembled together, such as to make it possible to remove them after disassembly and not demolition. An aphorism perfectly in line with the world of modern outdoor furniture, more and more eager to evoke the energy and forms of nature made with all sorts of materials. Transforming the garden and the outdoors into a botanical wonder that intrigues, amuses and leaves us enchanted is the goal, but we must be careful to choose the right design.

Modern outdoor gazebo: which cover to choose?

Shape, style, colors and materials used will play an important part in the final look. So, let's start with the design. For a period, house, in a historic center or in the countryside, such as a trullo or a farmhouse, perhaps near a swimming pool, a clean and minimalist design remains the best solution. White or graphite color, it can be perfect to give a sense of modernity while maintaining a historical soul.

For example, Shelter by Unopiù is the self-supporting pergola with a powder-coated aluminum structure that provides two types of cover: with adjustable motorized aluminum slats with radio control, or with waterproof fabric.

Adjusting the inclination of the slats allows you to find the right ratio between light, ventilation and temperature, ensuring maximum comfort at any time of the day.

The total closure of the slats allows to obtain good protection from the rain, to enjoy the outdoors even in extreme situations.

The version with integrated LED lighting includes 9 warm white spotlights.

The possibility of adjusting the intensity of the light from the spotlights gives the pergola a certain scenographic effect, since external lighting always remains a problem to be solved in such structures.

Pergolas and outdoor gazebos: a completely new idea

For more versatile situations, perhaps in which it is not necessary to install a structure that is too sturdy, you can opt for a more flexible and dynamic design, consisting of a fixed unit and one (or two) mobile units, with wheels, to extend and move it anywhere as you wish.

To be more functional, it is completed with different types of roofing: panels in impregnated Nordic pine strips, bamboo cane mats and micro-perforated fabric.

There are also securing brackets to keep it safe in case of strong wind.

Beautiful, safe, versatile and innovative: the right opportunity to describe a totally new exterior.

A tent for every occasion.

On the other hand, when you have a balcony or a small terrace to organize, the solution could be even lighter, creating a nice arrangement through a freestanding or wall-mounted curtain.

For example, an awning with extendable arms and rot-proof fabric, anti-mold and hydro / oil repellent that considerably reduces the irradiation and heating of the underlying environment allowing a reduction in air conditioning costs and therefore energy savings inside the home.

Printed in Great Britain
by Amazon

42114405R00076